STAR TEACHERS

STAR TEACHERS

the
Ideology
and
Best Practice
of
Diverse Children
and
Youth in Poverty

Dr. Martin Haberman

Published by the Haberman Educational Foundation in association with
NorthEast Magic Consulting.
Text Design and Photography by Ryan Cameron
Copy Editor - Grace Bezanson
www.habermanfoundation.org

ISBN:0-9761856-0-6

To Delia Stafford

Pioneer and leader
in selecting the
teachers and
administrators
the children of
America deserve.

Table of Contents

STAR TEACHERS

Introduction

Issues of race and ethnicity undergird every problem and solution in this volume. There is no separate chapter or section on multicultural education, diversity, issues of equity and justice, the impact of segregation on schooling, or maintaining access and excellence in American education. Such a chapter would support the notion that race and ethnicity is just one of many issues that explain the miseducation of fourteen million children in poverty. It is true that there are many explanations for our failing urban schools, e.g. inadequate funding; the advantages to various constituencies of maintaining and enlarging the bureaucracies of the urban school districts; maintaining present housing patterns; the political, economic and social benefits of miseducating other people's children; the benefits to universities of maintaining a system of failed teacher education; the benefits to the states for maintaining control over licensure; the benefits to the testing, textbook, and other industries which do business with schools; the benefits to those seeking to attain or remain in political office by promising to improve schools; the benefits to those classes and groups who understand that securing high quality education requires maintaining a bottom half; and all the constituencies who hold jobs in these failed systems. In every city in America the local school district is the largest single employer and as such is the economic engine that fuels the city and in many cases, the entire metropolitan area. Destroying these bureaucracies is a simple-minded advocacy when one realizes the number and extent of the beneficiaries. To have a separate section on "race and ethnicity" as just one of several explanations for maintaining failed urban school systems would be to make precisely the wrong argument. Issues of race and ethnicity comprise the core, the heart, the essence of the explanation for why our urban schools systems are protected and enlarged, even while they deteriorate to ever lower levels. The theories and research dedicated to explaining how racism is integral to the fabric of American society and to the socialization of every American have already been written—many times. And since schools reflect, rather than change society, it is only possible to understand schooling by first understanding the history and benefits of perpetuating racism.

STAR TEACHERS

This volume deals with symptoms and effects, not fundamental causes. Its purpose is to share what star teachers do to rescue children who are in the process of having their lives destroyed by miseducation. The solutions proposed i.e. getting better teachers who will do the specific things stars do, will accomplish three things: it will produce more children of color who learn more and who can compete for places in high quality schools and universities; it will open up teaching to more minority teachers who at present are seriously under-represented in the teaching force; and it will enable individual, failing schools to be transformed into effective ones, even though they function in the midst of failed district bureaucracies. Implementing my solutions will not transform entire failing urban school districts into successful ones; it will have little if any effect on racism, classism, or sexism in America.

It is neither accidental nor unexplainable that the schools serving students of color are also the schools with the greatest teacher turnover, with perpetual shortages of teachers, with more teachers engaged in custodialism rather than instruction, with the greatest number of teachers recommending suspensions and expulsions, with the greatest number of teachers recommending children be labeled as having handicapping conditions, and with the greatest number of attacks on teachers. The inability of teachers to relate to children, leads them to quit or fail and to students being miseducated. Why would a teaching force comprised predominantly of white women, who are monolingual, teach within fifty miles of where they were raised, and who attended small town, suburban and parochial schools have difficulty relating to diverse children and youth in urban poverty? The answer to this question has been well documented for decades. This volume recognizes that institutionalized racism is the root cause of miseducation and focuses instead on solutions.

In my city, approximately half of the African American and Latino students graduate from high school. I believe these horrendous rates are even lower because they do not include middle school ghosts who never make it into high school and who simply disappear after middle school. Still worse, is the fact that these graduation rates are not the lowest for students of color in the 120 major urban districts; many cities have fewer high school graduates of color. Compare this dismal miseducation with the graduation rates of students having handicapping conditions in the United States as a whole. In 2003, the

U.S. Dept. of education reported the following graduation rates for students with handicapping conditions as follows: learning disabilities 62%, language impaired 66%, mentally retarded 40%, emotionally disturbed 40%, multiple disabilities 48%, hearing impairments 68%, orthopedic impairments 68%, visual impairments 73%, autism 47%, blindness, 48%, and traumatic brain injury 65%. The average high school graduation rate for all categories is 62%. Stated simply, an American student who has been officially labeled as handicapped in some serious way which prevents him/her from learning has a better chance of graduating from high school than a student of color in one of America's major urban school districts.

My expectation is that American society will continue to improve in its treatment of ethnic minorities…but too slowly. Meanwhile, the schools serving diverse students in poverty will continue to worsen. Generation after generation of children cannot continue to be held hostage awaiting "transformers" and "change agents" to change the culture of poverty schools reflecting an inequitable society. My work represents a rescue business now, not a design for schools in the best of all non-existent worlds. I am pleased to give voice to the ideals and behaviors of star teachers who save so many lives everyday. This volume is dedicated to them.

Preface

On September 11, 2001, terrorist attacks in New York, Pennsylvania and Virginia claimed the lives of over 2,795 innocent civilians. But every day of the school year an average of 7,000 innocent civilians drop out of high school and very few take notice. America's greatest crisis is a silent one. While a majority of these youngsters are white, African America and Latino students are conspicuously over-represented. By the end of the school year as many as 500,000 tenth to twelfth graders will have "disappeared". My estimate is that, this horrendous statistic is matched by an equal number of those who never appear in any drop-out data because they have never made it into high school. They are the victims of failed middle schools using high stakes testing as an admission barrier into failing high schools.

9/11 clearly identified who were the perpetrators and who were the victims. In death by miseducation the blame for failing urban school districts is placed on the victims and their families who are accused of perpetrating their own demise. 9/11 evoked new national priorities and new ways of reaching them. Miseducation generates the same tired slogans and applies the same failed solutions even more assiduously. 9/11 brought forth a rebirth of patriotism and togetherness against those who would seek to destroy our concept of unity. Death by miseducation evokes an equally powerful commitment to preserve our way of life by making success in school a personal, rather than a common, good. In response to 9/11 America has committed itself to making significant changes in the way we will live. In response to death by miseducation America remains committed to protecting archaic, failed urban school districts from any significant change.

Fourteen million diverse children in poverty represent the overwhelming majority of the miseducated. The seven million in urban poverty, disproportionately represented by children of color, attend school in the 120 largest school districts. Every one of these districts is a failing school system in which greater size correlates positively with greater failure. Every miseducated child represents a personal tragedy. Each will have a lifelong struggle to ever have a job that pays enough to live in a safe neighborhood, have adequate health insurance, send their own children to better schools than they went to, or have a decent retirement. In most cases their lives are limited to dead end jobs, or wasted away in street violence or prison. Living in the midst of the most prosperous nation on earth, the miseducated will live shorter lives characterized by greater stress and limited life options.

Miseducation is, in effect, a sentence of death carried out daily over a lifetime. It is the most powerful example I know of cruel and unusual punishment, and it is exacted on children innocent of any crime. Most Americans avoid the personal tragedy aspect of this massive miseducation by not sending their own children to school in these failing urban districts. This includes a majority of the teachers who work in them! In effect, those with options cope with miseducation as a personal tragedy by fleeing the major urban districts in order to protect their loved ones from the contamination of miseducation. While flight can appear to be a successful strategy for coping with miseducation as a personal tragedy, it does not address the question of how miseducating other people's children on this massive scale affect the survival of the total society. Every three years the number of dropouts and pushouts adds up to a city bigger than Chicago. For how long can a society continue to create cities the size of Chicago every three years filled with "no hopers" and still survive as either a free or a prosperous nation?

The question of why a society that defines itself as caring, compassionate and committed to equal opportunity can continue to educationally destroy the life chances of millions of its own children is extremely difficult to understand and even harder to explain. When the dimension of being willing to risk our very survival as a nation is added, one can only conclude that most Americans perceive benefits from this miseducation that outweigh the damages they see being inflicted on individuals and society. This volume will focus on the ideology and practice of star teachers who function effectively even in the midst of failing schools and school districts.

Part One: The Nature of the Setting

Chapter I
Causes of the Teacher Shortage

Between the years 2000 and 2010, approximately 2,200,000 teachers, representing more than half of America's entire teaching force, will be hired. Most will be new teachers needed to serve more than 14 million diverse children in urban and rural poverty. The phenomenon of an urban school district needing thousands of teachers surrounded by suburbs and small towns where there are hundreds of applicants for one position has been well documented for over half a century. Several factors contribute to this "shortage" of teachers where they are needed most.

First, the length of an average teaching career is now down to eleven years. Teachers who pursue lifelong careers in the classroom are now clearly the exception. Second, the majority of those who graduate from traditional education programs never take jobs as teachers. For example, in 1998 seventy-one percent of those graduated and certified by Wisconsin colleges and universities did not take jobs as teachers. In 2001, sixty-one percent of the newly certified graduates did not take teaching jobs. This lower figure does not mean more teachers entered classrooms, however, since the total number produced in 2001 had declined by almost 20%. These non-teaching certified graduates frequently referred to by many as "fully qualified" don't take teaching positions because the jobs are primarily in urban schools serving diverse children in poverty. For what and for whom then are these graduates "fully qualified"? The licenses issued them contain no codicils or reservations such as "is prepared to teach white children not in poverty in small towns or suburban school districts." All fifty states issue only unrestricted, universal licenses pronouncing the bearers qualified to teach all children of a given age, or all children in a given subject matter, or all children with a particular handicapping condition.

The staggering percentage of the newly certified choosing to not waste his/her own time or the children's time is a second reason for the shortage. This is actually a benefit since potential quitters and failures do not inflict themselves on children in desperate need of competent caring teachers. Newly certified graduates not taking jobs is also a clear indication that the bearers of these licenses are much more honest about themselves and their lack of competence than those who prepared them and who insist on pronouncing them "fully qualified". In 1999, the SUNY system prepared 17,000 such "fully qualified" teachers. The number who applied for teaching positions in New York City that year was zero. The young white adults who comprise over ninety percent of the traditionally trained teachers simply don't want to or cannot relate to diverse children and youth in urban poverty.

The third reason for the teacher shortage is the number of beginners who take jobs in urban schools but fail or leave. Using data from the National Center for Educational Statistic's School and Staffing Survey, a respected researcher concluded: "School staffing problems are primarily due to excess demand resulting from a revolving door—where large numbers of teachers depart for reasons other than retirement." This churn of teachers into and out of schools, serving diverse children in poverty, results in about half of new teachers leaving urban districts in less than five years. In my own city half of the new teachers hired annually are gone in three years or less. Many quit in the first year. Another way to state this condition is to consider the impact on children. A class of predominantly white students has an eighty percent chance of having the same teacher all year; a class of predominantly African American students has a fifty percent chance of having two or more teachers in a year.

The fourth major reason for the teacher shortage in urban schools is the shortage of special education teachers. This shortage is exacerbated by the practice of many suburbs, small towns, parochial and private schools contracting out the education of their children with special needs to nearby urban school districts. This not only increases the teacher shortage in urban districts but raises costs. For example, my state and many others make deductions in state aid to the urban district for every special education class not taught by a certified special education teacher. This costs the school district in my city over two million dollars annually. No state imposes such a fiscal penalty when a district employs uncertified teachers in math, science or any other area of chronic shortage.

A fifth reason for the teacher shortage results from greater entrance level career opportunities now available to women outside of teaching at the time of college graduation. Many, however, soon discover glass ceilings and can only advance in limited ways. After age thirty this population includes many who decide to make more mature decisions than they did at age twenty and become teachers of diverse children in poverty.

The sixth reason for the shortage deals with college graduates of color who now have greater access into a larger number of careers than in former times. As with the population of women who perceive greater opportunity for careers in higher status jobs with greater financial reward than teaching, this population, also frequently experiences glass ceilings after age thirty. African Americans comprise fewer than six percent of all undergraduates in all fields and substantially fewer who decide as youthful undergraduates to pursue traditional university-based programs of teacher education. But as career changers after aged thirty, college graduates of color, particularly women, become a primary source of teachers for diverse children in poverty in urban school districts.

The continuing and worsening teacher shortage is exacerbated by conditions in special fields such as math and science. Math and science teachers leave at a higher rate than others. They tend to be men seeking better opportunities in other fields. While the causes of this shortage have some distinctive dimensions, they are not discussed separately but are included in the overall analysis. The solutions proposed for the general shortage will also impact these high need specializations.

The desperate shortage of special education teachers deserves further comment. The knowledge base purporting to explain child development, how children learn and what constitutes normal behavior offered in traditional programs of teacher education is derived from the field of educational psychology where the focus of study and analysis is the individual child not the culture. What is regarded as normal behavior is based on what white American school psychologists and teachers believe to be normal behavior and

5

development. For example, future teachers are taught that it is not normal for children to sit quietly all day. In my city there is a large population of Hmong children who sit quietly all day and are a source of great concern to their teachers, who place more credence on psychological definitions of normal, than they do on what they see acted out in front of them all day, everyday, by perfectly normal children of a different culture. It is not accidental that in my city with 89,000 children in public schools that there will soon be 20,000 children, mostly African American and mostly male, identified as emotionally disturbed, cognitively disabled or having some other handicapping condition. The fact that parents in poverty are enticed by state and federal programs for financial aid, if they agree to have their children labeled as handicapped, is little known and rarely mentioned. Depending on the particular handicap with which a child is labeled, parents may receive as much as $400 per month. In cities the size of mine there may be over one hundred school psychologists assisted by even more Diagnostic Teachers processing more than one thousand referrals from classroom teachers every year. In effect, in cities such as mine, school psychologists would have us believe that two out of nine of our children are abnormal. Given the present rate of referral, by 2012 twenty-five percent or one out of four of our children will be labeled as handicapped in some way. In Massachusetts twenty-eight percent of the African American school population is already labeled as handicapped in some way. Imagine what would happen in a white suburb or small town if the parents were told that one out of every four of their children was abnormal!

The hegemony of psychologists over the definition of normal becomes alarming when you understand that no state gives anthropologists, sociologists, linguists or any other professional the legal power to decide who is normal and what constitutes normal behavior. It should be remembered that four, state-certified psychologists swore under oath that, based on his responses to the Minnesota Multiphasic Personality Inventory, Jeffrey Dahmer was sane and capable of making normal moral judgments. The fact that he made love to the twenty-two dead bodies he had murdered and had actually eaten many of them was ignored in favor of his psychological test scores and he was declared sane. The bizarre reality imposed by those licensed to determine who and what is normal is that the results of tests which are supposed to predict behavior are given greater credence than actual behavior. This explains why school children, once labeled in primary grades, are rarely, if ever unlabeled in upper grades even if they subsequently earn good grades or pass the eighth-grade tests for high school admission. In effect, "fully qualified" teachers prepared in traditional university based programs are systematically trained to view many low income and minority children as somehow lacking, deviant, or having special needs.

New teachers unable to connect with and manage their students typically blame the children and their families, rather than face the inadequacies in themselves. Trapped by biased, limited definitions of how a normal child might develop, behave and learn language, they will inevitably recommend psychological assessments for children they cannot relate to and manage. School psychologists not distinguishing between "normal" and "desirable" then provide the backup test scores and psychological evaluations to "prove" that these children are incapable of functioning normally.

Studies of teacher quitters and leavers most commonly cite poor working conditions and difficult children as the most common reasons for leaving. Other reasons frequently cited include: overwhelming workload, discipline problems, low pay, little respect, lack of support and clerical workload. Reasonable people have good reason to question the validity of these responses, the maturity of the leavers making these responses and the quality of the teacher preparation offered those who give these reasons for leaving. Are we really to believe that even youngsters fresh out of teacher education programs have no idea that teachers' salaries are low until after they take jobs and actually receive their first paychecks? Are we really to believe that even new teachers are unaware of the media attacks and the public criticism of urban poverty schools until after being employed in them? Are we seriously to believe that new teachers have no idea before taking a position that working as a teacher will require an hour or two of planning time every night? Or, that there would be records to keep, papers to grade and parents to see People who work in offices, stores, factories, beauty salons and drive taxis, and who have not completed 60 credits of education courses and student teaching, are well aware of these factors as the typical working conditions of teachers. Indeed, interviews of high school students indicate quite clearly that even adolescents are well aware of these factors as the normal working conditions of their teachers. Quitters and failure teachers who offer these reasons for terminating their employment and those who accept and analyze these responses as authentic explanations make the findings of studies on why teachers quit or fail highly problematic.

While poor working conditions contribute to teacher losses, the in-depth interviews I have had with quitters and failures from schools serving diverse children in urban poverty over the past forty-five years reveal other explanations for leaving than those gleaned from superficial questionnaires, surveys and brief exit interviews. Our final classroom observations of failed teachers also support the existence of more basic reasons for leaving than those gained from typical exit interviews. Leavers are understandably chary about having anything on their records that they believe might make it difficult for them to get a reference or a future job. They are also savvy enough to try and not say things that might make them appear biased or prejudiced toward children of color or their families. It takes an hour or longer for a skilled interviewer to establish rapport, trust and an open dialogue in order to extract more authentic and less superficial reasons for why teachers leave. For example, the failure/quitter's identification of "discipline and classroom management problems" as the reason for leaving takes on new meaning when you understand what the respondent really believes. In typical surveys when quitters/failures mention the challenge of working with "difficult" students this comment is simply noted or checked or counted. In in-depth interviews, where rapport has been established, this cause is amplified by leavers into more complete explanations of why discipline and classroom management are difficult for them. They make statements such as, "I really don't see myself spending the rest of my life working with these children." or "It's clear that these children don't want me as their teacher." When the reason for the disconnect between themselves and the children is probed further, leavers frequently make statements such as the following: "These kids will never learn standard English," or "My mother didn't raise me to listen to 'm.f.' all day," or "These children could not possibly be Christians," or "These kids are just not willing or able to follow the simplest directions." Comments which may have at first appeared to indicate a simple, straightforward lack of management skills on the part of a neophyte can now be recognized as actually representing much deeper issues. Rather than a simple matter, which can be corrected by providing a few tips on classroom management, we have now uncovered an irreconcilable chasm between the teachers and their students. Teacher attrition increases as the number of minority students increases. Quitter/

failures cannot connect with, establish rapport, or reach diverse children in urban poverty because they do not respect and care enough about them to want to be their teachers. These attitudes and perceptions are readily sensed by students who respond in kind by not wanting these people as their teachers. Contrary to popular debates on what teachers need to know to be effective, teachers in urban schools do not quit because they lack subject matter or pedagogy. Quitter/failures know how to divide fractions and how to write lesson plans. They leave because they cannot connect with the students and it is a continuous draining hassle for them to keep students on task. Shortly after their hiring, leavers are emotionally and physically exhausted from struggling against resisting students for six hours every day. In my classroom observations of failing teachers, I have never found an exception to this condition. If there is a disconnect between the teacher and the students, no mentoring, coaching, workshop, or course on discipline and classroom management can provide such teachers with the magic to control children they do not genuinely respect and care about. In truth, graduates of traditional programs of teacher education can be termed "fully qualified", only if the definition is limited to mean they can pass written tests of subject matter and pedagogy. Unfortunately, while knowledge of subject matter and pedagogy are absolutely necessary, they are not sufficient conditions for being effective teachers of diverse students in urban schools. Knowing what and how to teach only becomes relevant after the teacher has connected and established a positive relationship with the students.

Many who give advice on securing the teachers needed to solve the shortage frequently assert that these children need to be taught by the "best and the brightest." Unfortunately, the typical criteria used to define "the best and the brightest" identify the precise individuals most likely to quit and fail with diverse students in poverty. The majority of early leavers have higher I.Q.'s, GPA's, and standardized test scores than those who stay; more have also had academic majors. Teachers who earn advanced degrees within the prior two years leave at the highest rates. Those who see teaching as primarily an intellectual activity are eight times more likely to leave the classroom. In 1963, my Milwaukee Intern Program became the model for the National Teacher Corps. In the ten years (1963-1972) of the Corps' existence, approximately 100,000 college graduates with high GPA's were prepared for urban teaching in the largest, longest study ever done in teacher education. While many stayed in education moving up to various administrative jobs, fewer than five percent remained in the classroom more than three years. The fact that the shibboleth "best and brightest" still survives proves that many prefer to maintain their pet beliefs about teacher education in spite of the facts. In reality, the criteria typically used to identify the "best and brightest" are powerful, valid predictors of failure/quitters.

While effective teaching of diverse children in poverty has some intellectual and academic aspects, it is primarily a human relations activity demanding the ability to make and maintain positive, supportive connections with diverse children, school staff and caregivers. The "best and the brightest" might be more appropriately used to refer to practicing teachers who actually demonstrate the propensity to connect with and cause diverse children in poverty to learn, rather than as a descriptor of college youth with high GPA's who do well on written tests of teaching. There is substantial evidence that teachers, who have greater knowledge of the subject matters they teach, and more advanced skills of English communication will have children who learn more. But it is only after the teacher has demonstrated the ability to relate to diverse children in poverty that the teacher's knowledge becomes transferable to students.

This raises the more basic issue of whether future teachers (or veteran teachers) can be taught to connect with diverse children in poverty or whether this attribute can only be learned through mature reflection about one's life experiences after one has had some life experiences. If it is, as I believe, the latter then it is an attribute that must be selected for and not assumed to result from completing university coursework as a late adolescent or young adult. Indeed, substantial evidence indicates that college courses and direct experiences reinforce rather than change teacher education students' prejudices and abilities to relate to diverse children in poverty. Because of selective perception, students in university training programs merely "see" what they are predisposed to "see" in their direct experiences and coursework. Open students become even more open and narrow students merely reinforce their limited views of the world. In effect, teacher education produces graduates more predisposed to believe whatever they believed when they began their programs. This also happens during in service programs for veteran teachers. The dynamic by which trainees see what they want to see, makes

10

selecting the right people a more productive approach to preparing teachers than assuming that training programs are treatments powerful enough to transform the ideology of teachers unable to relate to students. Given the need for teachers with the belief systems and the predispositions to effectively relate to diverse children in poverty in dysfunctional school bureaucracies, there can no longer be any question that selecting those with the appropriate dispositions determines the usefulness of any subsequent teacher education program offered them.

Chapter II
Some Pertinent History of Teacher Education
Which Helps Explain the Current Shortage

The first normal school training teachers in America was a private one started in 1823 by a Pastor Samuel Hall in Concord, Vermont. The program was a three year follow-up to the elementary grades and was based on his "Lectures on Schoolkeeping." Due to the efforts of Horace Mann and others, Massachusetts established the first state normal school in 1837. Girls were admitted at 16 and boys at 17. The program was one year in length and involved being drilled in the fundamentals. Students also took studies in surveying, physiology, the Constitution and history of the Republic. Connected with the normal school was a model school, where the master would demonstrate rudimentary pedagogy to the neophytes. All future teachers were also instructed in Christian piety and morality.

During this period itinerant male school masters moved about the country and were contracted by communities to keep school for a few months. By the Civil War women were replacing men as teachers for several reasons. They worked for less money than men, they were regarded as more capable of morally training the young, they needed gainful employment if they did not marry, and their role as purveyors of basic skills and moral behavior was seen as the level of work women were capable of doing. Between the Civil War and WWI, the growth of normal schools burgeoned and became extended into post secondary training programs of one and then two years.

Between 1890 and 1920, 30 million immigrants, mostly low income white Europeans, came to a United States. Those already here were extremely fearful of being overrun by non-English speakers who they believed could not function as productive citizens without some basic schooling. The highest

13

level of education achieved by most of these immigrants was sixth grade or less until the migration subsided in the 1920's. While the urban schools took on the mission of making Americans, teacher education remained a pastoral pastime essentially ignoring the urban schools to which most of the immigrants sent their children.

Except for the western states, every state opened normal schools and some states had over ten. During the 20th century these normal schools were extended into four year teachers colleges offering baccalaureate degrees. After WWII they became state colleges offering comprehensive majors not limited to teaching. The old two year normal schools did not die easily and in Wisconsin the last one remained open until 1969. Along with this expansion of teacher education into multi-purpose universities came over 550 laboratory schools attached to these colleges where the latest methods of pedagogy were developed and demonstrated with white children of university faculty members and local professionals.

The knowledge base in teacher education developed after WWI with the growth of educational psychology and educational philosophy. But neither the psychologists nor test experts professionally descended from E.L.Thorndike, or the progressives seeking to implement the work of John Dewey, ever recognized the existence of African Americans. Also ignored were those in urban poverty and people in any ethnic group not seeking to abandon their culture and language and melt into the mainstream. The progressives, philosophers and citizenship educators were all clearly defeated by the educational psychologists who claimed to have universal constructs regarding the nature of child development, the nature of learning and the nature of evaluation and research. The constructs of educational psychologists still exert hegemony over the basic knowledge base used in colleges and universities preparing teachers today.

During this same period the land grant institutions, comprising the flag ship institutions of their respective state's public higher education systems, also took on the responsibility of preparing teachers. Today, with the exception of states whose higher education was developed differently in response to later statehood, we see a pattern of states with major land grant institutions now deeply involved in teacher education and a larger number of state colleges that were formerly the single purpose teacher training institutions still preparing most of the teachers. In recent years private institutions have begun contributing some teachers to urban school districts, but these tend to be small numbers in boutique programs and not the major source of teachers for urban districts.

A few very vital points of this history are relevant to the current analysis and need to be kept in mind in order to more clearly understand why traditional programs of teacher education do not prepare enough teachers for diverse children in urban poverty.

• Teacher training institutions were purposely and systematically located across rural America (where their state college descendents remain today), because their clients were white, unmarried farm girls who needed employment.

• A great number of such normal schools were needed to ensure that female teachers would not work further than fifty miles from home, could easily return home for holidays and summer work, and that the teachers being trained would likely be of the same religious and ethnic background as the children they would be training in morality and the abc's.

• The notion that school teaching is the appropriate work of young, single women has been imbedded in American culture for more than 180 years. The perception that even married women are less appropriate than single women has been reinforced during periods of economic depression when married women in many urban districts were laid off.

• There were very few public normal schools started in urban areas. A few exceptions existed in St. Louis and Detroit but these closed or were subsequently included in larger multipurpose institutions. New York City, with the largest population of children in the country, never had a single publicly supported normal school, but the State of New York opened twelve in rural areas.

• There can be no question that teacher training in America was developed as a rural phenomenon for the children of Europeans of primarily Protestant background. Catholics tended to cluster in the cities and attend parochial schools where teachers were from religious orders and were not normal school graduates. Beginning in the 20th century, however, large numbers of Catholic women became teachers in urban public schools and now constitute the majority of teachers in many eastern and midwestern public urban school systems even today.

• The need for teachers who could be effective with African Americans, other children of color, children in urban poverty and non-European populations was never a consideration in the development of the knowledge base in American teacher education.

• The knowledge base purporting to explain normal child development, how normal children learn and what constitutes normal behavior that is offered in traditional programs of teacher education is derived primarily from educational psychology where the unit of study and analysis is the individual…white individuals. Other ways of understanding and explaining human behavior that reflect cultural constructs and ways of knowing are still very marginal additions to state requirements for approving university based teacher education programs, e.g. a course in Multicultural Education.

What is the import of these trends? After one understands even a few of the basic facts surrounding the development of teacher training in America, it is extremely naïve to raise questions such as why teacher education is not relevant to diverse children in urban poverty, or why teacher education does not provide more teachers who will be effective in teaching all children, or why teachers who complete traditional programs of teacher education do not seem to be able to relate to all children. It was never the intention of teacher education in America to prepare teachers to teach all the children. And based on an analysis of the current output of teachers who seek to avoid teaching where they are needed most and who will not stay longer than a brief period if they do accept positions in poverty schools, it is entirely reasonable to conclude that the historical and cultural truths regarding teacher training in America still explain and predict the functioning of university based teacher education today.

Chapter III
The Rationale for Recruiting and Preparing Adults as Teachers of Diverse Children in Urban Poverty

The crisis in urban school schools serving diverse children in poverty is worsening. The persisting shortage of teachers who can be effective and who will remain in urban poverty schools for more than brief periods is a major cause of this crisis. The benefits of securing and preparing more effective teachers are several: fewer children will be damaged; more children will learn more; and if teachers are placed as groups into failing schools these schools will be turned around. At the same time it must be recognized that getting better teachers and even turning failed individual schools into successful ones will not transform the 120 failed urban school district bureaucracies currently miseducating seven million diverse children in poverty. Selecting new populations of teachers prepared in new ways will provide more islands of success in failing districts. The belief system and behavior of effective urban teachers makes it clear that they are focused on their students' learning and development. They are driven to help each youngster be as successful as possible. They do not go into or stay in teaching because they want to function as educational change agents, community organizers or system reformers. Their raison d' être is their students, first and last.

It is also important to understand how and why some teachers succeed in spite of the debilitating working conditions created by failed urban school bureaucracies. These organizations are not only likely to improve but worsen, creating even more negative conditions which impinge on teachers' work and children's learning. Indeed, there is a perverse irony here: as more effective teachers are recruited, selected and prepared the pressures to break up or have states takeover failed urban districts decreases. A pernicious, debilitating school bureaucracy is, in effect, made to look workable as it secures and retains more teachers who literally drain and exhaust themselves in order to function in spite of the systems in which they must work. But while good teachers can transform failed schools into successful ones, they cannot transform entire failed urban districts. At the district level, issues dealing with federal mandates, state laws, funding formulas, school board politics, superintendent turnover, central office mismanagement and local culture must be resolved before systemic change can occur. Because schools reflect rather than change society and because too many powerful constituencies benefit from these failed urban districts, it is highly unlikely these issues will ever be dealt with in ways that transform failing urban school bureaucracies into organizations that function in the interests of children, teachers and parents. Nevertheless, recruiting, selecting and preparing the teachers needed by diverse children in poverty should be vigorously pursued because they can and will rescue individual children and transform individual schools.

Much can be done to get the teachers needed. Too many decades have already passed and too many youngsters have been driven out, miseducated or been underdeveloped awaiting the change agents who would have us believe they can transform urban school districts and their debilitating impact on teaching and learning. This is a critical issue because defenders of traditional teacher education argue that before their excellent programs of teacher education can be held accountable for their "fully qualified" graduates to succeed and remain in poverty schools, the debilitating conditions of work must be changed. This analysis argues that securing and retaining effective teachers can and must happen now because the children need them now and because the conditions in urban school districts are quite likely to get even worse.

The Nature of Adolescence and Adulthood as it Pertains to the Education of Teachers for Diverse Children in Poverty

There is an extensive literature on the nature of adolescence and adulthood. Much of it is focused on the life stages of people in general while a lesser amount refers to the stages of teacher development. Almost all of this literature comes from psychologists or writers who use psychological constructs and suffers from the same ethnocentricity that characterizes the knowledge base in teacher education. But since over 90% of those in traditional university programs of teacher education are white youth from working class and middle class families, the characteristics attributed to these young adults is most relevant and worth noting.

University magic occurs when students graduate from high school. They are declared "adults" by their respective states and by the universities in which they enroll. Bestowing this status frees the university from having to pay any serious attention to students' natures or to their stage of development. The notion that it is critical to know the nature of the learners and the nature of their development in order to teach them is of no concern and completely ignored by university faculty. In place of stages of development, higher education relies on contrived categories of status representing the university organization, e.g. freshman, undergraduate, full time, or GPA level. The areas in which youth force universities to respond to their developmental needs are in extra-curricular activities such as food service, health care, and rules related to housing and safety. It is no accident, therefore, that those out-of-class activities which do respond to the nature and level of their development frequently cause more change in students than their formal studies.

Late adolescents and young adults are still struggling with the issue of self-identity, fighting off peer pressure, asserting independence from family and grappling with their own struggle to achieve meaning and purpose in life. They are haunted by questions like, "Will I find someone to love me?" "Will I be able to earn a living?" "How do I gain independence from my mother and still show her I love her?" The period of the 20's is frequently identified as a time of impatience and idealism. "Now" becomes the focus and "me-ness" i.e. what I want now, an obsession. Those in their early twenties are infatuated with ideals but have not experienced or observed enough of life to provide a workable basis for understanding themselves or the world. This often leads to impetuous behavior regarded by authority figures as rebellious or lacking in judgment. In American society these and other insecurities are normal concerns and explain the almost complete self absorption of youth as they seek to answer the basic questions of identity. Teaching, on the other hand, is a continuous effort to inspire confidence in others. Juxtaposing the demands of teaching with the natural and common needs of young adults in American society highlights the inappropriateness of the match. It is the needs of the children not the teachers that must be the focus of the teaching-learning relationship. The willingness and ability to empathize with and nurture others is the essence, the very soul of teaching. These attributes are present in very few college youth focused on themselves. Because the work of the teacher requires building self-esteem in others not in trying to find oneself, there is no stage of development less appropriate for training teachers than late adolescence and young adulthood.

On the other hand, mature adults have a strong and reasonable sense of who they are and are self-accepting. Such adults are sufficiently confident to be motivated by intrinsic rather than extrinsic rewards as they engage creating learning activities. The benefit of a university education to mature adults is that they are able to integrate their personal experiences with theory, research, logic and a system of morality and apply them to the persistent problems of living in a free society. Educated adults consciously test common sense and unexamined assumptions against various ways of knowing. Freed of the adolescent's need to realize parental expectations and the pressures of equally immature peers, adults seek to reconcile their inner direction with the social good. Terms such as integration, generativity and self-realization have all been used to define adults who have reached the level of aligning their proclivities with the demands of society. They seek self enhancement by contributing not by merely taking or getting.

In Lawrence Kohlberg's theory of moral development individuals move through the following stages:

I. concern about obedience,
II. satisfaction of needs and wants,
III. concern with conformity,
IV. concern with preserving society,
V. concern with what is right beyond legalities,
VI. concern with universal ethical principles.

According to Kohlberg, only 10 per cent of those in their twenties ever attain Stages V. or VI. His findings indicate that "college students are capable of employing reasoning at these levels yet rarely do so."

THE RATIONALE FOR RECRUITING AND PREPARING ADULTS AS TEACHERS OF DIVERSE CHILDREN IN URBAN POVERTY

Erik Erikson's theory of human development includes eight stages: trust vs. mistrust (first year); autonomy vs. doubt (ages 2-3); initiative vs. guilt (ages 4-5); industry vs. inferiority (ages 6-11); identity vs. role confusion (ages 12-18); intimacy vs. isolation (18- through young adulthood); generativity vs. self-absorption (middle age); and integrity vs. Despair (old age). For Erikson generativity can only occur after individuals have resolved the issue of intimacy. Generativity is most common in young parents but can also be found in individuals who are actively concerned with the welfare of young people and making the world a better place for them to live and work. Those who fail to develop generativity fall into a state of self-absorption in which their personal needs and comforts become their predominant concern. Researchers building on Erikson's model have extensively studied college students to determine at what point they develop a sense of their own identity and found that only 22 per cent achieve this level.

Other researchers have described college youth as lacking commitment to any philosophy or set of beliefs, living for the moment and not delaying gratification. Jean Piaget equated his fourth stage of formal operations with adulthood. At this level individuals engage in abstract thinking, prepositional thinking, combinatorial thinking, hypothetical-deductive thinking, thinking ahead, metacognitive thinking and self reflection. Piaget found that college students rarely reach this level of thinking.

Kitchener followed college youth through their undergraduate years and found them beginning as moral and intellectual absolutists, moving to a stage of relativism when any opinion is as good as any other and ending up in a search for identity with most never getting beyond the middle stage of relativism.

Other models of development focus on stages of development and the nature of knowledge sought in each. Late adolescents and young adults typically use their direct experiences in support of absolutism, they then move through the stage of weighing conflicting perceptions (relativism) and conclude with a more mature view of reality and multiple ways of knowing. This last stage is seldom or ever reached in college youth. It is ironic that youthful college students, who believe so much in the value of their own experiences as the best way to learn, undervalue the experiences of the children they teach by limiting them to texts and vicarious experiences.

Teacher educators bombarded by preservice students' fears and apprehensions regarding classroom discipline are well aware of the childlike stage in which many about to be certified find themselves. There is seldom little if any concern with higher levels of thinking, or human development, or with subject matter, or with how issues of social justice and equity can be infused into school curricula. Indeed, a strong resistance develops to pursuing these issues. As preservice students move toward graduation, certification and their first teaching positions, there is a marked narrowing of their interests and concerns. The complex problems of teaching and learning are ignored as they fall under the spell of one grand obsession: "Will I be able to control the class?" This is the overriding concern of the new graduates awarded universal licenses by all states and heralded by university based teacher educators as "fully qualified."

There is no value in simply getting older. But serious reflection upon one's life experience is more likely to result in individuals reaching higher levels of development. Having families, work experiences and sustained careers provide individuals with rich and varied experiential material to integrate into their cognitive and emotional development. The potential of teacher growth through reflection is great, so too are the dangers for those individuals who have difficulty reflecting accurately upon their strengths and weaknesses. Clearly those with more life and work experiences have more with which to build up their perceptual repertoires. Reflection is more likely to be of greater value to mature adults because it requires meaningful life experiences to draw upon.

Ultimately, my belief in the need for greater teacher maturity is based on the fact that star teachers serving diverse children in urban poverty perform at a very high conceptual level. If we perceive teaching as essentially a mindless set of jejune tasks (e.g. the 19th century school-marm teaching the abc's and giving directions all day) then the level of knowledge needed by practitioners would be of little importance. Indeed, many urban school districts have given up trying to find teachers who can think at all and have mandated that instruction be done by reading from scripts. On the other hand, if we believe teaching requires higher-order thinking skills, advanced knowledge of subject matter and the ability to apply abstract concepts such as equity and justice, then the teachers' cognitive and affective development becomes the crucial determinant of success. There have been multiple studies (over 200) in many countries which have found that there are four general developmental abilities which are highly related to success in any field: 1) empathy, 2) autonomy, 3) symbolization, and 4) commitment to democratic values. All four of these correlate with greater maturity. In the American sample there was an inverse correlation between SAT scores and level of maturity.

Paul Pintrich's landmark meta analysis of the research summarizing learning and development of college students and its implications for teacher education has never been utilized by traditional university-based programs of teacher education. Reasonable people cannot read Pintrich's summary of what is known about human development and learning and still focus on young adults as the primary source of teachers. Using any respectable theory of human development leads to the same conclusion. For white, working and middle class females growing up in American society there is no more inappropriate stage of life to prepare for teaching than young adulthood… and for comparable males their personal development and the demands of teaching are an even greater mismatch. What do these scholarly summaries about teachers' levels of development mean when translated and applied to the real world? We are supposed to believe that a system of traditional teacher education which would take a young, immature white male from a small town in Wisconsin, put him through a traditional program of teacher education, graduate, certify and declare him "fully qualified" at age 22, is engaged in a perfectly reasonable activity. Further, we are to believe that it would be a good idea for this young man to come to the Milwaukee Public Schools (or to any urban district in America) and be hired as a teacher because he is now a professional practitioner who can shape the mind and character of a seventeen year old African American girl with a child and a part-time job trying to make a place for herself in the world. Or, that he has the knowledge, skills and predispositions to help a Latino five year old make sense of the world. Or, that he has the competencies needed to help a young adolescent survive the throes of puberty and the peer pressure to drop out.

The best that can be said about such a monumental disconnect between the nature of who is in teacher preparation and the demands of practice in urban schools is that we should be grateful to the majority of these young men and women who never take jobs. They know and are willing to declare their inadequacies more truthfully than the faculty who trained them. There are two reasons why traditional programs continue to focus on training the wrong population as teachers for diverse children in poverty. The first is that faculty members simply don't know better. Over ninety percent of regular school of education faculty (not adjunct, ad hoc, or clinical appointees), are individuals who have not been teachers in poverty schools for three years or longer. The majority have never taught at all in any of the 120 major urban school systems. They simply don't know what is required of effective teachers in failing school districts. Second, education faculty perceive their clientele to be the teacher education students who pay the tuition that pays their salaries, not the diverse children and youth being miseducated by their graduates. University faculty can maintain the fiction that they are preparing teachers for the real world because they are not held accountable for how effective their graduates are, or whether their graduates ever even take jobs. As beneficiaries of a system that are paid for by the late adolescents and young adults who take their college courses, it is not difficult to understand why university faculty do not accept the fact that maturity should be the sine qua non of admission into teacher training. Self interest is infinitely more powerful than the evidence.

Success in school is a matter of life and death for children and youth in poverty. Young adults in our society do not typically hold any jobs involving life and death. From air traffic controllers to brain surgeons to bus drivers, jobs that involve life and death are clearly understood to require judgment as well as skill. Traditional university programs are able to continue training the wrong population for teaching because neither they nor the general public really believe that success in school for diverse children in poverty is a matter of life and death.

Chapter IV
How Do Mature Teachers Cope with the School Bureacracy?

More mature teachers demonstrate persistence in how they teach students and how they cope with the bureaucracy. Rather than feel persecuted, as many young teachers do, mature teachers with work experiences outside of schools quickly discern the weaknesses and contradictions in the plethora of rules, regulations and policies that characterize school bureaucracy. Their work and life experiences lead them to see that the school district organizations are far from well-oiled machines. While there may be rules and procedures for everything, there is typically an inadequate administrative span-of-control to oversee compliance. In my training programs, for example, we overtly train beginning teachers not to read everything that is put into their mailboxes. We teach them how to sort the barrage of messages and paper dumped on them at the start of the school year so that they only take time from teaching to comply with the most urgent, legal demands; similarly with classroom interruptions, which average 125 per week in urban schools. Our training provides specific teacher strategies for cutting down on classroom interruptions and dealing with only the very few that are essential.

Administrators and secretaries frequently behave as if the teachers are there to help them run the building and complete reports for central office. They do not act as if they believe that they hold support jobs which should be focused on helping teachers teach and students learn. Beginner teachers must find ways to obtain the assistance they need without allowing their teaching time to be wasted on paperwork and out-of-class concerns. Mature teachers with work experiences are much easier to mentor in this regard because of their previous work experiences in a wide range of other bureaucracies.

One of the items on our Star Teacher Selection Interview deals with burnout. Younger teachers' responses to the causes of burnout more frequently resemble those of quitter/failure teachers. They do not expect to ever experience burnout. They perceive burnout as something that only happens to teachers who lack dedication. They have no concept whatever that burnout is caused by working hard in depersonalized organizations, thick with regulations, which impact negatively on teaching and learning. Mature adults, on the other hand, see burnout as a natural consequence of working in any organization. They believe burnout can happen to anyone including themselves. Candidate's answers to this question predict who is more likely to survive in failing, highly bureaucratized school districts.

Mature teachers network with other teachers for the purpose of gaining personal and professional support. This is the most effective antidote to burnout. By developing allies (teachers, principals, secretaries, custodians, aides) who support their initiatives they develop a support group that insulates them from feeling isolated. They also seek and obtain greater involvement and support from parents.

Mature teachers search for ways in which the bureaucracy can actually be used to help them and their children. Experienced insiders in any large system can be very effective at gaining more freedom for themselves. They learn about rules and procedures which are little known or seldom used that offer relief from bureaucratic oversight. They know about and make useful connections with people in the district office who are willing to help them. Savvy teachers seek out these cracks in the bureaucracy and utilize them in the interests of their children. Examples include how to secure a piece of equipment or extra supplies, how to get permission for a field trip or special activity, or how to qualify for a small grant. Negotiation, compromise and conflict management skills are successful responses used by mature adults when coping with any bureaucracy. Such skills can be learned from experience, but mature teachers who come into the classroom already equipped with such skills can be immediately more helpful to their students. They are also more likely to survive the first difficult years. It must be remembered, however, that effective urban teachers only use such skills to improve learning opportunities for their children. They do not finesse the system for personal gain.

The willingness to be held responsible for one's actions and to accept accountability for children's learning is clearly related to maturity. These are attributes that are vital in schools where constant testing has become the norm. Teachers of diverse children in poverty must be accountable for student achievement in spite of negative conditions in the lives of children over which they have no control. As teachers they must also function under horrendous conditions of work over which they have no control. Successful practitioners accept being held accountable. In every occupation that involves the life and death of the clients, practitioner effectiveness is clearly related to maturity, judgment and the willingness to accept responsibility.

Ultimately, mature teachers are able to cope with the school bureaucracy effectively because they are also successful in relating positively to the children. As superiors, colleagues and aides become dependent on star teachers for managing children others cannot control; they are less likely to harass them with inhibiting rules regarding their teaching.

Mature, effective teachers are able to cope in failing urban school districts because their focus is on their students. They devote their energies before, during and after school to their students. They do not see themselves as change agents. They do not typically take the lead in change efforts that threaten the system. They are more likely to look for "elbow room" from the bureaucracy only to try things in their classrooms that will help their students learn. One sign of maturity is the wisdom to know which conditions of work are amenable to change and which must be lived with.

Chapter V
Where Do Urban Schools Get Their Beginning Teachers?

Although the typical age of college graduates has risen from age twenty-two to age twenty-six, it is still generally true that most of those preparing to teach are college age youth, that is, late adolescents and young adults. This analysis is not an advocacy for preventing all such individuals from becoming teachers but to shift the balance. The current ratio of beginning teachers remains approximately eighty percent youngsters below age twenty-six who are full-time university students to twenty percent older, "non-traditional" post baccalaureate adults in alternative certification and on-the job training programs. Given the fact that greater maturity predicts greater effectiveness and staying power in urban poverty districts, this balance should be reversed so that the majority of beginning teachers would be adults over age thirty with experience in the world of work. Denigrating labels such as "retreads" or "career changers" indicate the power of the misconceptions and stereotypes regarding the age at which it is generally believed that individuals should become new teachers. My best estimate is that of the approximately 500,000 traditionally prepared teachers under age twenty-six produced annually, fewer than fifteen percent seek employment in the 120 major urban districts serving approximately seven million diverse children in poverty. This represents approximately seventy-five thousand of the colleges and universities annual teacher output. The research based on my Star Teacher Selection Interview indicates further that of this fifteen percent who are willing to apply to work in urban school districts that only one in ten of those under age twenty-six will stay long enough (three years) to develop into effective teachers in these schools. When researchers report that fifty percent of beginning teachers of diverse children in poverty are gone in less than five years, it must be remembered that this is fifty percent of the fifteen percent who deign to accept positions in these school districts. What this means is that the 1,250 traditional programs of teacher education who prepare over one-half million youngsters under age twenty-six as teachers, actually supply the 120 largest urban school districts with about 1.5 percent of their annual teacher output in the form of teachers who stay. While this is obviously a very small output from traditional teacher preparing institutions, it does include a small bloc of young people who do have the potential for teaching diverse children in urban poverty and for whom the doors of the profession should remain open. But should this population of young teachers remain the predominant body of future teachers, or should school districts be looking for other constituencies from which to draw and develop the teachers America needs? If a factory made television sets but only 15 percent of them could be turned on and only 1.5 percent were working after three years   would we insist on keeping this production model and complain about the terrible places the plugs are located, or would we be emphasizing new ways to make television sets?

The reality of the situation is that more mature adults who are uncertified college graduates have for years been a major source of the teacher supply in every urban school system. For decades, urban school systems have kept their schools open by using pools of local adults who are college graduates from fields outside of education and who serve as long term substitutes and provisional teachers. In my relatively small city there are several hundred such teachers who keep the schools going, while the "fully qualified" are hired each September and quit during the school year. Many school districts now pay the tuition of their long term substitute and provisional teachers who then work their way through traditional teacher certification programs after they have been teaching in the districts for many years. This is most common in special education and other high need specializations. District support reaches outrageous proportions when, for example, the New York City schools pay $12,500 per teacher for thousands of interns to complete certification programs at local colleges after they have already worked as responsible teachers of record in the NYC schools. These are millions of dollars which should be spent on children and youth, not on post baccalaureate certification programs which add no discernible value to teachers' performance. New York State (as well as many other states) now question why their well-endowed systems of public higher education use tax payer funds to graduate "fully qualified" teachers who do not take jobs, or who cannot succeed in schools where they are needed most. If the State University of New York system graduates 17,000 "fully qualified" teachers annually and none apply to work in New York City, questions are inevitably raised about the use of taxpayer funds. As more school districts spend more funds which were intended for schools on teacher education at the same time that the overwhelming number of "fully qualified" graduates of traditional teacher education programs do not take jobs where they are needed most, (or quit and fail if they do), questions are inevitably raised in state legislatures regarding the continuation of state support for unproductive traditional programs of teacher education. With the nationwide deficits in states' budgets it is inevitable that more questions will be raised about state support for preparing teachers who don't or can't teach. Texas gave up on its non-productive system of teacher education in 1985 by limiting the amount of state support to schools of education to 18 hours of coursework in education. In 2003, three states gave up on traditional forms of certification entirely and replaced it with a system of written tests for certifying college graduates with any major. More states will do the same. It is already clearly evident that there is a two-track system of teacher certification: traditional university programs for young, female adults under twenty- six seeking to teach in small towns and suburbs; and on-the-job training for mature college graduates from all fields without formal coursework in education preparing on-the-job to teach diverse children in poverty. Both groups will also be expected to pass state mandated tests.

It is quite clear that the current and future teachers of diverse children in urban poverty will come from non-traditional populations of adults trained on-the-job These may be programs offered by university-school partnerships or by the urban school districts themselves. Those who cannot recognize this reality are those who have a stake in not wanting to be convinced that traditional programs of teacher preparation are not relevant to the urban districts. It is difficult for university based teacher educators to maintain that they know best how to prepare teachers when they don't do it. The excuse is that "we are preparing excellent teachers in sufficient numbers but cannot be held accountable for their performance or their staying power because the conditions of work in urban schools drive them out." In truth, traditional teacher educators could put all of the alternative certification programs they rail against out of business immediately if they were able to prepare teachers for the real world, rather than for the best of all non-existent ones. Many superintendents rationalize their preference for hiring young "fully qualified"

Chapter VI
Will the Conditions of Work for Beginning Teachers Improve or Worsen?

While I have argued that teachers leave primarily because they cannot connect with children, it is necessary to recognize that the conditions under which beginning teachers work in urban schools are horrific and drive out not only those who should have never been hired but many who have the potential for becoming effective teachers and even stars. The option is whether the strategy of waiting for change agents to transform the conditions under which teachers work in failing urban school districts makes more sense than recruiting and training more mature people who can succeed in schools as they presently are. Over the last half century the conditions of work have continued to deteriorate in the 120 largest districts. Efforts to transform these failing districts have not worked in any of them. How much longer must children and youth in these districts continue to wait before they get teachers who can relate to them and teach them effectively?

In my own city we train beginning teachers who are often expected to work under conditions that are medieval: some classrooms are without windows; many classes have over thirty students including six or more with handicapping conditions; insufficient, outdated textbooks; no dictionaries or paper; no access to a copier that works; no computers connected to the internet; no running water or any materials in "science" rooms; no closet that locks and no hook to hang up a teacher's coat. Not all these conditions exist in every classroom, but they are frequent enough to be very familiar. Teachers in my city spend an average of $600 dollars per year of their own money on supplies. We have teachers who use their own funds to buy chalk. When I recently asked a principal to provide a teacher with some chalk he replied, "The teachers knew how much money we had for supplies and they chose to use it up by January. What do you want from me?" Observing the equipment, supplies and materials that urban teachers typically have to work with frequently leads one to question whether these teachers are working in the United States of America. I recently visited schools in New York City on behalf of the New York State Department of Education. The classrooms were exactly like the ones I was in as a child in the same city sixty-five years earlier. The only difference I could see was that there was an electric clock on the wall. In this financial and cultural world center I observed many caring, well intentioned beginning teachers whose only teaching material was a blackboard or paper already used on one side. In the schools I visited, the teachers had essentially the same teaching materials as teachers in Afghanistan, except that the buildings had indoor plumbing and central heating. Many of our urban schools function as isolated third world outposts in the midst of a 21st century technological society.

Being processed through an urban district's cumbersome personnel systems for an initial appointment, securing an assignment to a particular school and classroom, and then meeting the never-ending paperwork and clerical demands wear even highly motivated people down in short order. In my own city beginning teachers are hired by computer interview and by filing paper credentials. Imagine never speaking to an individual face to face and being hired as a teacher! The message conveyed to beginners is that they are essentially invisible and unimportant as individuals. But this is not the full extent of the bureaucratic depersonalization. Focusing on test scores to the exclusion of any thoughtful teaching and learning, requiring endless paperwork and allowing people to teach in classrooms with an average of 125 interruptions per week create exhausting pressures. The mindless, overpowering bureaucracies of urban school districts seem organized for the express purpose of driving out those who care the most, and retaining only the strong insensitives i.e. those who can put up with the negative conditions of work and not become stressed out because they really don't care about the children or their miseducation. Advocating what "should be", conducting status studies, writing more media stories, or merely complaining about conditions of work will not change the nature of failing urban school districts. The critical question is whether these conditions will improve or worsen? My prognosis that conditions will continue to worsen is based on an examination of the five conditions of work most commonly cited by teachers: salaries, safety, class size, principals and testing.

WILL THE CONDITIONS OF WORK FOR BEGINNING
TEACHERS IMPROVE OR WORSEN?

Salaries. In my city a single mother with two or more children (a typical profile of the pool that is likely to stay in urban teaching) will earn a starting salary low enough to meet the state's poverty criterion and is entitled to food stamps. In the future, teacher salaries will not increase in real dollars and are likely to fall further behind others of comparable education in other occupations. Much worse than the annual rate of inflation is the out-of-control cost of health care which triples every decade. Urban school districts will negotiate greater contributions from teachers to help cover these costs and will still be forced to put whatever monies they might have used for salary raises into health care. In my own city the teachers' benefit package is already sixty-one percent so that a beginning teacher paid $30,000 per year actually costs the district $48,300. By 2012, a very conservative estimate is that the benefits package will be eighty percent. This means that a beginning teacher paid $40,000 will cost the district $72,000 per year… and this assumes that the teachers will be paying for a greater share of their health care, thereby, decreasing their real income further. Since health care costs are not likely to be contained it is unlikely that teachers will ever receive raises of any significance or even stay abreast of inflation. Neither states nor local school districts have the means to infuse the massive support required to alter this trend.

School Safety. The amount that urban districts pay for school safety personnel and equipment will continue to increase. This not only diverts funds from educational purposes but seriously alters school climate. Schools serving diverse students in poverty have become custodial rather than educational institutions in the major urban districts. In many urban middle and high schools there is already more invested in hall cameras, safety equipment and safety personnel than in computers or computer assisted instruction. As more staff time is directed to issues of control it casts a pall over the self concepts of beginning teachers who prefer to think of themselves as educators rather than safety personnel. It is not likely that in the future urban schools will deemphasize their custodial functions.

Class Size. This condition has a great impact on beginners. It will continue to move in two directions. In a few states which mandate smaller classes, usually for primary grades, there will be a sharp increase in the teacher shortage but smaller classes for those who take jobs in these states. Prohibitive costs make it unlikely that the goal of reducing class size beyond primary levels is one that will be realized. In most urban districts class size will increase in response to budget cuts and higher birth rates among the urban poor. These increases in class size will be worst in middle schools where teachers face the most serious behavior problems and where most of the students who will not make it into high school are retained for an extra year or longer. In urban middle schools, teachers work with between one hundred and one hundred fifty students daily. These schools are likely to be places where large classes make the conditions of work extremely difficult. Caring teachers recognize that this is the last chance for many youth to make it into high school or drop out, and as a result they work especially hard. The conditions of work in urban middle schools make it more likely that the teachers who stay for longer than five years are likely to be the strong insensitives rather than those who are caring and committed.

Supportive Principals. There is a growing shortage of effective urban school principals. An increasing number of urban districts now hold the principal accountable for raising test scores on an annual basis. Raising these expectations for principals cuts down on the pool of those who can be effective in such demanding roles. It is noteworthy that beginning teachers frequently cite "having a supportive principal" as the most critical factor in their professional development. There is a continuing and growing shortage of school leaders who can function effectively in African American and Latino communities. It is not uncommon for major districts to fire or transfer as many as fifty principals in one year but then not have replacements that are any more effective. The obstacle to turning this situation around is that future principals are drawn from the ranks of former teachers and assistant principals in the same failing urban districts. Unless there is an increase in the pools from which future principals are drawn their quality will not increase. Over half the elementary schools in many of the urban districts are now officially designated as Schools in Need of Improvement under the Leave No Child Behind law. This means that the teachers and assistant principals who comprise the pool from which future principals are drawn may never have worked for, or ever observed, a principal functioning as an accountable, instructional educator leading an effective urban school. As the shortage of effective principals increases and more schools are officially designated as failing, the demands and expectations for what the principal must accomplish increases. There is growing expectation that the effective urban principal can no longer be a building manager but must be the instructional leader of a non-profit community organization. Raising expectations regarding this leadership role are necessary but will deepen the shortage. Without sufficient models of success to emulate and limiting new appointments to only those who have worked in the district, the most likely prognosis is that tomorrow's principals will fail in the same ways and at the same rate as today's. This makes the likelihood that beginning teachers will be getting more support from an increasing pool of more effective principals highly problematic.

Tests. The number of tests taken by students in urban schools is not likely to diminish. District and state mandates have now made testing a fact of life for urban teachers. In some districts the curriculum is so tightly aligned with the mandated tests that teachers actually follow scripts to cover all topics in the exact ways the students will be tested for. This is a critical condition of work for many beginners who naively believed that as teachers they would function as professional decision-makers rather as test tutors. The very strong likelihood is that the pressures felt by teachers to prepare their children for tests will intensify since so many will be assigned to schools officially designated as failing or in need of improvement.

On the positive side there has been an increase in several conditions which beginners rate as critical conditions of work. First, there is more teacher teaming than in the past. This means that beginning teachers have greater access to veteran teachers' ideas and experiences. Second, there is more mentoring of beginning teachers by experienced teacher with released time. Both of these factors are expensive because they involve greater staff costs and while implemented in a few urban districts they are cut back in most others. If these five working conditions (salaries, safety, class size, tests and principals) are cited by urban teachers as the most critical, and if all five are likely to worsen, is it a more responsible strategy to continue to prepare teachers in traditional ways and wait for the working conditions in the schools to improve, or to prepare new populations of teachers who can succeed in failing urban school districts which are likely to get even worse?

Chapter VII
Securing Teachers

Traditional teacher education cannot provide the great number of teachers who can be effective and who will remain in urban schools for more than brief periods of time. Securing the teachers needed for the real world will require new forms of teacher education employing new procedures: a) recruiting mature college graduates from all fields and from the various careers; b) selecting only individuals whose belief systems predispose them to see teaching and schooling as a means of fostering equity and justice for diverse children in poverty; c) preparing candidates while they function as fully responsible, paid teachers of record in schools serving diverse children in poverty; d) providing a support system that includes coaching from skilled mentors; e) giving them technology that connects them instantly to resources and problem solving; f) offering professional studies which are closely aligned with the actual behaviors candidates must perform as teachers; and g) evaluating and recommending candidates for licensure after they have demonstrated they can effect children's learning. Using these procedures, we have trained diverse, mature college graduates from all fields of study for the Milwaukee Public Schools since 1990. Seventy- eight percent of them are minorities and ninety-four percent of them are still teaching after a decade. Securing the teachers that diverse children in urban poverty need and deserve requires taking some initiatives which are in opposition to the current practices and culture of traditional teacher education.

1. The clients of colleges and universities preparing teachers are not the students in these programs, but diverse children in poverty in urban schools who need effective teachers. If universities were held accountable for their graduates more candidates would be failed or would self select out before they are officially dubbed "fully qualified". So long as university faculty regard their clients as those who pay the

tuition (and their salaries), children and youth will not get their teachers from traditional programs.

2. The great shortage of urban teachers does not mean that standards should be lowered but that they must be raised. Teachers who will be effective and who will remain are individuals who have in-depth knowledge of subject matter, who can connect with diverse children in poverty and who can function under extremely adverse working conditions. In traditional teacher education, whether or not the graduates can relate to diverse students in a dysfunctional school bureaucracy is only determined after they have been declared "fully qualified", hired by a school district and given responsibility for the learning of children.

3. Candidates should not be admitted into programs of teacher education because they have passed traditional selection criteria at a college or university. Urban school districts should first process candidates through their selection procedures. Only those candidates the district indicates they would be willing to hire and guarantee a position should be admitted to programs of preparation.

4. The locus of preparation must be urban school classrooms in which the candidates function as teachers of record. The various pools of adults who can be recruited, selected and prepared to be effective in urban schools envision themselves changing careers in order to function in the role of teachers. They are not willing to take on the role of students in teacher education programs and have demonstrated clearly, over decades that they will not be recruited if their primary role is to become college students rather than teachers. This means alternative certification programs, intern programs, and on-the-job training programs must be used to recruit and prepare mature candidates.

5. The traditional system of young college students deciding they would like to be teachers of a particular age or subject matter and then seeking employment after graduation is completely irrelevant to preparing teachers for diverse children in poverty. The starting point for creating the pools of teachers to be trained in the various specializations should be based on projections of teacher needs in particular urban school districts.

Then those teacher education programs which can fill the specific school needs for the various teacher specializations required should recruit, select and prepare candidates to meet those specific needs.

6. For teachers to remain and be effective, their training program cannot focus on universal truths, i.e. the supposed universal nature of child development, teaching and learning. Neither can it be preparation focused on professional schools modeling best practice, since these are nonexistent worlds. From the outset, candidates' preparation must focus on serving particular groups of children from specific local cultures attending schools in a particular urban district. Preparing candidates for no place in particular and then declaring them able to teach all children everywhere will only perpetuate the current system of "fully qualified" graduates not taking jobs, quitting or failing. There is no shortage of teacher candidates whose primary motive is to secure licenses which will enable them to be hired in any state. The need is for teachers for specific urban schools, serving particular constituencies. Mature adults from a specific urban area who begin with a focused local, urban commitment are more likely to not only succeed, but to remain in urban schools.

7. The tradition of waiting for young undergraduate students to apply to a university to be prepared as teachers must be replaced with aggressive and targeted marketing programs directed at pools of local, adult college graduates, particularly those of color. Nationwide and traditional forms of recruitment by urban school districts competing with each other for a limited pool of young minority graduates need to be replaced by strategies which focus on mature residents of the local metropolitan area. Local churches and faith–based community organizations are basic to the recruitment of African American and Latino applicants. While women and mothers with children in the very same school systems in which they would like to become teachers are the primary target; ways of reaching local male pools must also be utilized. New ways of explaining the work of a teacher in an urban school district need to be an integral part of honest, realistic marketing that lets applicants know what they are getting into from day one. Signing bonuses and similar inducements for enticing reluctant applicants who lack commitment to diverse children in the particular urban area are counterproductive and

should be discontinued.

8. Specific attributes of great (star) urban teachers should guide the selection of new teachers into preparation programs. Traditional criteria, which predict success in college (e.g. GPA) should be ignored. The real admission criteria should be interviews of applicants which compare their ideology to star teachers followed by observations of candidates actually relating to children and youth. These are the two most powerful predictors of success for teachers of diverse children in urban poverty.

9. College graduates should be the primary source for the new pools of teacher candidates who need to be recruited. There should be no limitation on the fields of study which these candidates have completed. Grade point and other traditional university admission criteria are irrelevant. They predict success in subsequent coursework and quitter/failure teachers of diverse children in poverty.

10. It is counterproductive to focus on or even include masters degree studies during the first year of any internship, residency or on-the-job training program. First year teachers must focus their complete time and energy on learning to teach and must never be sidetracked into completing masters courses during this very hectic period. Their first year must be spent on their students and their own development as teachers not completing term papers for graduate classes. Substantial research and experience makes it clear that earning a masters degree is most helpful after beginning teachers have demonstrated the ability to relate to students and offer effective instruction.

Considering the factors beginning teachers say they need or would like, versus those they regard as debilitating, the likelihood is far greater that the negative conditions for beginning teachers in urban schools will not only continue but worsen. What this means for securing teachers who will stay and become effective is clear. While all constituencies must do everything possible to try and improve the conditions under which beginning urban teachers work, children cannot be held hostage waiting for school changes that never come. The need is for teachers who can be effective with today's children and youth in today's schools. We must not accept the pious position that it is unfair or even immoral for beginning teachers to have to function in today's schools, and therefore, teacher educators cannot be held accountable for whom they select and train until the urban schools are first transformed. There are real children, spending the only childhood they will ever have going to failing schools everyday. Demanding that failing school districts improve before effective teachers can be prepared to work in them will sacrifice the education of another 14 million children in poverty. Change agents have been notoriously unsuccessful over the last half century. The wisest, most pragmatic policy assumes that whether failing schools stay the same or get even worse, it is necessary to recruit and prepare caring, knowledgeable teachers who will make a difference immediately.

Part Two:

The Nature of Traditional Urban Teaching Practices

Chapter VIII
The Pedagogy of Poverty Versus Good Teaching

Why is a "minor" issue like improving the quality of urban teaching not generally included among the popular reform and restructuring strategies? There are several possibilities. First, we assume we know what teaching is, that others know what it is, that we are discussing the same "thing" when we use the word teaching, and that we would all know good teaching if we saw it. Second, we believe that since most teachers cannot be changed anyway, there must be other more potent, teacher-proof strategies for changing schools than improving teaching. Third, why bother with teaching if research shows that the achievement test scores of poor and minority youngsters are affected primarily by their socioeconomic class and ethnicity?

Observing urban classrooms, it is possible to find examples of almost every form of pedagogy: direct instruction, cooperative learning, peer-tutoring, individualized instruction, computer assisted learning, behavior modification, pupil contracts, media assisted instruction, scientific inquiry, lecture-discussion, tutoring by specialists or volunteers, and even the use of problem-solving units common in progressive education. In spite of this broad range of pedagogic options, however, there is a typical form of teaching that has become accepted as basic instruction. This style of teaching encompasses a body of specific teacher acts and has become more common each year since I first noted it in 1955. Now, half a century later, a teacher in an urban school in the first decade of the 21st century who does not engage in these acts will be regarded as not engaged in teaching. Performing these acts for most of each day is considered prima facie evidence that the teacher is teaching. The specific acts which comprise urban teaching are the following:

- giving information,
- giving directions,
- making assignments,

- reviewing assignments,
- asking questions,
- monitoring seatwork,
- assigning homework,
- reviewing homework,
- punishing non-compliance,
- settling disputes,
- marking papers,
- giving tests,
- reviewing tests,
- giving grades.

This is the basic menu of teacher functions. It characterizes the "teaching" of all subject matters at all grade levels to all children including those with handicapping conditions. A primary teacher might "give information" by reading a story to children while a high school teacher might read to the class from a biology text. Interestingly, they both offer the same reasons for the act, "The students can't read the material for themselves" or, "They enjoy being read to." Taken separately, there is nothing wrong with these activities. There are occasions when any one of these fourteen acts might have a beneficial effect on learning. Taken together and performed to the systematic exclusion of other acts, they have become the pedagogic coin of the realm in urban schools. They constitute the pedagogy of poverty—not merely what teachers do and what youngsters expect but also what school administrators, parents, community, and the general public assumes teaching to be.

Ancillary to this system is a set of out-of-class teacher acts which include keeping records, conducting parent conferences, attending staff meetings, and performing assorted school duties. These out-of-class functions are supposed to support instruction but are performed in ways which support the pedagogy of poverty. In urban settings these out-of-class functions are actually euphemisms for activities that would be considered offensive if described truthfully. "Record keeping" refers to the systematic maintenance of a paper trail to protect the school system against any future legal action by the clients. Special needs, special classes, referrals, test scores, disciplinary actions, and analysis by specialists must be carefully recorded. Because the information that is gathered was determined to be necessary by school lawyers, reading student records is more likely to prejudice teachers than inform their instruction. The system regards the upkeep of these records as vital to its legal and financial survival. In many cities it is now common for special education teachers to spend more time recording what they are doing for special students and filling out time sheets than in actually performing the services they are keeping records about. "Parent conferences" refers to giving parents, who are perceived as poorly educated or otherwise inadequate, a chance to have things explained to them. "Staff meetings" refers to giving administrators opportunities to explain things to teachers who are perceived as poorly informed and otherwise inadequate. "Assorted school duties" refers to safety and monitoring activities that would be better performed by guards hired for such activities.

The pedagogy of poverty appeals to several constituencies:

1. It appeals to those who themselves have not done well in school. People who have been educationally brutalized are not rich sources of compassion. Those who have failed or generally done poorly in school have not had many models of great teachers. Typically, such casualties of poor schools believe they would have succeeded if only somebody had forced them to learn.

2. It appeals to those who rely on common sense rather than thoughtful analysis. It is easy to criticize humane and developmental teaching aimed at educating a free people as mere "permissiveness" and it is well-known to all with common sense that "permissiveness" is the root cause of our educational problems.

3. It appeals to those who fear minorities and the poor. Bigots are typically obsessed with the need to control "those" people.

4. It appeals to those who have low expectations for minorities and the poor. People with limited vision frequently see value in limited forms of pedagogy. They believe that at-risk students are best served by directive, controlling pedagogy. Direct instruction is now required in many urban districts.

5. It appeals to those who do not know the full range of pedagogic options available. This group includes most school administrators, almost all business and political reformers and even many teachers.

Star Teachers

There are essentially four syllogisms which undergird the pedagogy of poverty. Their "logic" is something like this: A. Teaching is what teachers do. Learning is what students do. Therefore, students and teachers are engaged in different activities. B. Teachers are in-charge and responsible. Students are those who still need to develop appropriate behavior. Therefore, when students follow teachers' directions appropriate behavior is being taught and learned. C. Students represent a wide range of individual differences. Teachers are trained to assess these differences. Therefore, ranking is inevitable so that some students will end up at the bottom of the class while others finish at the top. D. Basic skills are required for subsequent learning and living. Students are not necessarily interested in basic skills. Therefore, directive pedagogy must be used to insure that youngsters are compelled to learn their basic skills.

The Nature of Reform and the Pedagogy of Poverty

Unfortunately, the pedagogy of poverty does not work. Youngsters achieve neither what they are capable of learning nor minimum levels of life skills. The classroom atmosphere created by constant teacher direction and student compliance seethes with passive resentment that frequently bubbles up into overt resistance. Teachers burn out because of the emotional and physical energy that they must expend to maintain their authority every hour of every day. The pedagogy of poverty requires that teachers, who begin their careers with the self-perception that they are helpers, models, guides, stimulators, and caring sources of encouragement, transform themselves into directive authoritarians in order to function in urban schools. People who select themselves to become teachers do not do so because at some point they decided "I want to be able to tell people what to do all day and then make them do it!" The gap between expectations and reality means that there is a pervasive, fundamental, irreconcilable difference between the motivation of those who select themselves to become teachers and the demands of urban teaching.

For the reformers who seek higher scores on achievement tests, the pedagogy of poverty is a source of continuing frustration. The clear-cut need to "make" students learn is so obviously vital to the common good and to the individuals themselves that surely (it is believed) there must be a way to force students to accept the pedagogy and to work hard enough to vindicate the methodology. Simply stated, we act as if it is not the pedagogy which must be fitted to the students but the students who must accept a sacrosanct method.

In reality, the pedagogy of poverty is not a professional methodology at all. It is not supported by research, theory, or the best practice of superior urban teachers. It is actually a set of ritualistic acts that, much like ceremonies performed by religious functionaries, are conducted for their intrinsic value rather than to foster learning.

There are those who contend that the pedagogy of poverty would work if only the youngsters accepted it and would work at it. "Ay, there's the rub!" Students in urban schools overwhelmingly do accept the pedagogy of poverty and they do work at it! Indeed, any teacher who believes s/he can take on an urban teaching assignment and ignore the pedagogy of poverty will be readily crushed by the students themselves. Examples abound of inexperienced teachers who seek to involve students in genuine learning activities and are met with apathy or bedlam, while older hands who announce, "Take out your dictionaries and start to copy the words that begin with 'h'", are rewarded with compliance.

Reformers of urban schools occasionally try to raise their expectations beyond an emphasis on basic skills to the teaching of critical thinking, problem solving, and even creativity. But if the pedagogy of poverty will not force the learning of low level skills, how can it be used to compel genuine thinking? Heretofore, reformers have promulgated change strategies which deal with the level of funding, the role of the principal, parental involvement, decentralization, site based management, choice, and other organizational and policy reforms. At some point, they must reconsider the issue of pedagogy. If the actual instruction expected by school administrators and teachers and demanded by students and their parents continues to be the present one, then reform will continue to deal with all but the central issue: How might the quality of student learning be raised?

Star Teachers

The pedagogy of poverty is sufficiently powerful to undermine the implementation of any reform effort because it deals with how pupils spend their time, the nature of the behaviors they practice, and the bases of their self-concepts as learners. Essentially, it is a pedagogy in which learners can "succeed" without becoming either involved or thoughtful.

The Nature of Urban Children and Youth

In accepting a New York City Teacher of the Year Award, John Taylor Gatto stated that no school reform will work that does not provide children time to grow up or simply forces them to deal with abstractions. Without blaming the victims, he described the behavior of his students as lacking curiosity (having "evanescent attention"), being indifferent to the adult world and having a poor sense of the future. He further characterized them as ahistorical, cruel and lacking in compassion, uneasy with intimacy and candor, materialistic, dependent and passive—although they frequently mask the last two traits with a surface bravado.

Anyone who would propose specific forms of teaching as alternatives to the pedagogy of poverty must recognize that Gatto's description of his students is only the starting point. These are the attributes that have been enhanced and elicited by an authoritarian pedagogy and do not represent students' true or ultimate natures. Young people can become more and different, but they must be taught how. This means that two conditions must pertain before there can be a serious alternative to the pedagogy of poverty: 1) the whole school faculty and school community—not the individual teacher—must be the unit of change; and 2) there must be patience and persistence of application since students can be expected to resist changes to a system they can predict and control. Having learned to navigate in urban schools based on the pedagogy of poverty, students will not readily abandon all their know-how to willy-nilly take on some new and uncertain system which they may not be able to control.

For any analysis of pedagogic reform to have meaning in urban schools it is necessary to understand something of the dynamics of the teacher-student interactions in these schools. The authoritarian and directive nature of the pedagogy of poverty is somewhat deceptive about who is really in charge.

Teachers seem to be in charge, in that they direct students to work at particular tasks, allot time dispense materials, and choose the means of evaluation to be used. It is assumed by many that having control over such decisions makes teachers "decision makers" who somehow shape the behavior of their students.

But below this facade of control is another more powerful level on which students actually control, manage, and shape the behavior of their teachers. Students reward teachers by complying. They punish them by resisting. In this way students mislead teachers into believing that some things "work" while other things do not. By this dynamic, urban children and youth effectively negate the effects of their teachers' professional preparation and undermine the non-authoritarian predispositions which led their teachers to enter the field. And yet, most teachers are not particularly sensitive to being manipulated and shaped by students. They believe they are in control and are responding to "student needs" when, in fact, they are more like hostages responding to students' overt or tacit threats of noncompliance and ultimately, disruption.

It cannot be emphasized enough that in the real world, urban teachers are never defined as incompetent because their "deprived," "disadvantaged," "abused," "low income," students are not learning, but because they cannot elicit compliance. Once schools made teacher competence synonymous with student control it was inevitable that students would sense who was really in charge.

The students' stake in maintaining the pedagogy of poverty is of the strongest possible kind: it absolves them of responsibility and puts the burden on the teachers, who must be accountable for making them learn. In their own unknowing, but crafty way, students do not want to trade a system in which they can make their teachers ineffective for one in which they would themselves become accountable and responsible for what they learn. It would be risky for students to swap a "try and make me" system for one that says, "Let's see how well and how much you really can do."

STAR TEACHERS

Recognizing the formidable difficulty of institutionalizing other forms of pedagogy, it is still worthwhile to define and describe such alternative forms. The few urban schools which serve as models of student learning have teachers who maintain control by virtue of their ability to establish trust and involve their students in meaningful activities rather than by imposing some authoritarian system of classroom discipline. For genuinely effective urban teachers, discipline and control are primarily a consequence of their teaching and not a prerequisite condition of learning. Control, internal or imposed, is a continuous fact of life in urban classrooms, but it is completely interrelated with the learning activity at hand. Engaged students are not pr oblems.

Indicators of Good Teaching

Is it possible to describe a teaching approach that can serve as an alternative to the pedagogy of poverty? I believe there is a core of teaching acts that defines the pedagogy one finds in the classrooms of star urban teachers who have been recognized as exemplary. Unlike the directive acts that comprise the pedagogy of poverty, these tend to be indirect activities that frequently involve dealing with the creation of a learning environment. These teaching behaviors tend to be reflected more by what the students are doing than in the observable actions of the teacher. Indeed, teachers may appear to be doing little and at times may, to the unsophisticated visitor, seem to be merely observers. These acts of good teaching transcend all grade levels and subject matters.

Whenever students are involved with issues they regard as vital concerns, good teaching is going on. In effective schools the endless "problems"—the censuring of a school newspaper, an issue of school safety, a racial flare-up, the dress code—are opportunities for important learning. In good schools, problems are not viewed as occasions to impose more rules and tighter management from above. Far from being viewed as obstacles to the "normal" school routine, difficult events and issues are transformed into the very stuff of the curriculum. Schooling is living, not preparation for living. And living is a constant messing with problems that seem to resist final solutions.

Whenever students are involved with explanations of human differences, good teaching is going on. As students proceed through school they should be developing an increasingly greater understanding of human differences. Why are there rich people and poor people, able and disabled, urban and rural, multilingual and monolingual, highly or poorly educated? Differences in race, culture, religion, ethnicity, and gender are issues that children and youth reconsider constantly in an effort to make sense of the world, its relationships and their place in it. This is not "social studies." All aspects of the curriculum should deepen students' basic understandings of human differences as a pervasive fact of life.

Whenever students are being helped to see major concepts, big ideas, and general principles and not merely engaged in the pursuit of isolated facts, good teaching is going on. At all levels and in all subjects key concepts can be made meaningful and relevant. Students cannot be successful graduates without having at some point been exposed to the various forms of knowledge. Historians deal with the nature of sources, artists with texture, color and design. A fundamental goal of education is to lead students to develop the ability to use varied and competing ways of understanding the universe. Knowing how to spell or divide fractions is not enough.

Whenever students are involved in planning what they will be doing, it is likely that good teaching is going on. This planning involves real choices and not simple preferences such as what color crayon to use, or the order in which a set of topics will be discussed. Students may be asked to select a topic for study, to decide what resources they will need, or to plan how they will present their findings to others. People learn to make informed choices by actually making informed choices. Following directions—even perfectly—does not prepare people to make life choices and deal with the consequences of those choices.

Whenever students are involved with applying ideals such as fairness, equity, or justice to their world, it is likely that good teaching is going on. Students of any age, at all levels, can apply great ideals to their everyday lives. The environment, war, human relationships, and health care are merely a few examples of issues that students of all ages can be thinking about. Determining what should be done about particular matters and defending their ideals publicly gives students experience in developing principles to live by. Character is developed by students who have had practice and experience at comparing ideals with reality in their own lives and in the lives of those around them. Whenever students are actively involved, it is likely that good teaching is going on. Doing an experiment is infinitely better than watching one or reading about one. Participating as a reporter, a role player, or an actor can be educational. Constructing things can be a vital activity. Behavior leads to more powerful learning than passive listening. We need graduates who have learned to take action on their own behalf and on behalf of others.

Whenever students are directly involved in a real-life experience, it is likely that good teaching is going on. Field trips, camping, interacting with resource people, work and life experiences are all potentially vital learning activities. First-hand experience is potentially more educative than vicarious activity, provided it is combined with reflection.

Whenever students are actively involved in heterogeneous groups, it is likely that good teaching is going on. Students benefit from exposure to cultural as well as intellectual heterogeneity because they learn much from one another. Divergent questioning strategies, multiple level assignments in the same class, activities that allow for alternative responses and solutions all contribute to learning. Grouping in schools is frequently based on artificial criteria that are not used in life. Grouping can either limit or enhance students' self-concepts and self- esteem, and thus, has a powerful effect on present and future learning.

Whenever students are asked to think about an idea in a way that questions common sense or an assumption accepted as "good" by everyone, or relates new ideas to ones learned previously, or applies an idea to the problems of living, then good teaching is going on. Students are taught to compare, analyze, synthesize, evaluate, generalize and specify in the process of developing thinking skills. The effort to educate thoughtful people should be guided by school activities that involve thought. The acquisition of information—even of skills—without the ability to think is an insufficient foundation for living in a free, diverse society.

Whenever students are involved in redoing, polishing or perfecting their work, it is likely that good teaching is going on. Students can learn that doing things over is not punishment. It is in the act of review, particularly review of one's own work that important learning occurs. This may involve an art project or a science experiment as well as a piece of writing. The successful completion of anything worthwhile rarely occurs on one trial.

Whenever teachers involve students with the technology of information access, good teaching is going on. Teachers, texts, and libraries as they now exist will not be sufficient. Computer literacy—beyond word processing—is a vital need. Electronic learning must play an important part in the mix, even at the expense of customary practices. Today, students and educators alike can create, receive, collect, and share data, text, images, and sounds on myriad topics in ways more stimulating, richer and timelier than ever before.

Whenever students are involved in reflecting upon their own lives and how they have come to believe and feel as they do, good teaching is going on. Autobiography can be the basis of an exceedingly powerful pedagogy—one that is largely discarded after early childhood education. When critics dismiss my characterization of the pedagogy of poverty as an exaggeration, I am reminded of an immense sign hanging in an urban high school that has devoted itself totally to the acts I have called the pedagogy of poverty; "We dispense knowledge. Bring your own container." This approach assumes students are hollow vessels without personality, culture or a background of life experiences. Autobiographic activities are readily extended into studies of family, neighborhood and community. What could be more fundamental to subsequent learning than self-definition? Urban schools, in the way they narrowly structure the role of teacher and restrict the content to be taught, too frequently repudiate the students, their culture and their ethnicity. Good teaching is a process of "drawing out" rather than "stuffing in".

The Rewards of Not Changing

Taken individually, any of these indicators of good teaching will not transform a poor teacher into a good one. We all know individual teachers who have done some of these things for years. Taken together and practiced school-wide and persistently, however, these suggestions create an alternative to the pedagogy of poverty and can transform a failing school into an effective one.

Unfortunately, we must recognize that it may no longer be possible to give up the present authoritarianism which characterizes teaching in urban schools. The incentives for the various constituencies involved may well have conditioned them to derive strong benefits from the pedagogy of poverty and only unknown risk from the options.

In the present system teachers are accountable for only engaging in the limited set of behaviors commonly regarded as acts of teaching in urban schools; that is, the pedagogy of poverty. Students can only be held accountable for complying with precisely what they have specifically and carefully been directed to do. Administrators can only be held accountable for maintaining safe buildings, and parents only for knowing where their children are. Each constituency defines its own responsibilities as narrowly as possible to guarantee itself "success" and leaves to others the broad and difficult responsibility for integrating students' total education.

Who is responsible for seeing that students derive meaning and apply what they have learned from this fragmented, highly specialized, overly directive schooling? It is not an accident that the present system encourages each constituency to blame another for the system's failure. These constituencies have a stake in maintaining their present roles which, in effect, hold them unaccountable for educating skilled, thoughtful citizens concerned with issues of equity and justice.

Continuing to regard non-thinking, underdeveloped, unemployable youngsters as "adults" or "citizens" because they are high school graduates, or have passed the General Educational Development (GED) examination is irresponsible. Education will be seriously reformed only after we move it from a matter of some importance to a matter of "life and death," both for society and for the individuals themselves. The teachers who can educate a free people do not perform the mindless tasks commonly mistaken for teaching. They are practitioners of a moral craft. Graduates who lack basic skills may be unemployable and represent a personal and social tragedy. However, graduates who possess basic skills but are partially informed, unable to think, work in teams, or make moral choices are downright dangerous. Before we can make workers, we must first make people.

Chapter IX
Unemployment Training: The Ideology of Non-work Learned in Urban Schools

For many young people who live in poverty, moving from school to a decent job is about as likely as having a career in the National Basketball Association. Urban schools struggle and fail at teaching basic skills, but they are extremely effective at teaching skills that predispose young people to fail in the world of work. The urban school environment fosters a set of behaviors and beliefs that enables youngsters to slip and slide through middle school and high school but that also becomes the source of their subsequent failure. It is an ideology that is easily learned, readily implemented, rewarded by teachers and principals, and supported by school policies. Schools promulgate this ideology because it is easier to accede to students' street values than to try and change them.

The dropout problem in urban school districts—as catastrophic as it— is less detrimental than the active training that urban students receive for becoming unemployable. Urban youths are not just poorly prepared for work but systematically and carefully trained to be quitters and failures. And the "successful" youngsters who graduate from urban schools are the ones who have been the most seriously infected. They have been exposed to the ideology and have practiced the anti-work behaviors for the longest period of time; they have also been rewarded the most for practicing these non-work behaviors.

The fact that the ideology of unemployment is not a part of the formal curriculum does not make urban schools less culpable for its transmission. This curriculum is carefully taught and systematically rewarded in urban schools. The concepts which comprise this ideology follow.

STAR TEACHERS

Nowness. In urban schools, learning is offered in short, discrete jolts. The work on any given day is unconnected to the work of preceding or subsequent ones. Life in urban schools is composed of periods and days that stand on their own. If textbooks are never taken home and homework never completed (behaviors which are universal for urban males and almost universal for females by the time they have completed the elementary grades), everything that students are taught must be compressed and completed in stand-alone periods of less than one hour. And like their students, teachers and principals become conditioned to survive one period and one day at a time.

By focusing on what can be learned in one period or even during one activity within one period, urban schools claim to be "meeting the needs of urban students" who are frequently absent, late, suspended or newly transferred to the school. (In some urban schools it is common for student turnover between September and June to reach and even exceed 100%.) The rationalization is that with all this coming and going many students would always be playing catch-up if the lessons could not be completed in one period. Another rationalization for this disjointed curriculum is the large number of special programs which cause youngsters to be pulled out of classes. But the most common reason offered for "nowness" is the claim that students seldom remember anything they have been taught before. Thus, the introduction of any new concept or skill inevitably requires an extensive review of everything that preceded it.

For example, a middle or high school teacher might try to present a lesson dealing with the results of a recent election. But the teacher quickly discovers that almost no one in the class can explain the difference between the city, county, state and federal levels of government. At this point the teacher has two choices. To back up and spend the period re-teaching these distinctions, which were supposedly taught in 4th grade, or to go ahead with the lesson for the few who understand the distinctions. Some youngsters have learned to play dumb to keep teachers from teaching the lessons they have planned. In most cases, however, students have forgotten and are genuinely ignorant of even the most elementary concepts—things that teachers assume students know in order to offer the curriculum at their grade level.

UNEMPLOYMENT TRAINING: THE IDEOLOGY OF NON-WORK LEARNED IN URBAN SCHOOLS

Nowness is the operating norm of the urban school. A successful period is typically one in which students are expected to have neither prepared anything nor are expected to follow up in any way. In the absence of connections to past or future learning, most of what goes on in urban classrooms resembles television game shows.

On the program Jeopardy, viewers can tune in whenever they choose to and never be behind. There are always new words and new answers so that viewers need not remember the words used on previous days in previous shows. And best of all, the rules for playing are quickly reviewed anew each day. A viewer who tunes in for the first time knows as much as a person who has been watching everyday. There are no penalties for missing as many programs as one chooses. Anyone can show up at any time and play the game. Teachers encourage nowness because, like students, they are trying to get through each day with minimum hassle. But it is impossible for students to learn ideas of any real consequence or develop skills to any level of useful proficiency when nowness controls the conditions of teaching and learning. Real education is a process of building connections and scaffolding learning from elementary to more advanced levels. This process involves hard work. It is even harder work for teachers. By "going with the flow", teachers foster the dangerous misconceptions that connecting simple ideas to more advanced ones is something that teachers, not students, have to do and that the length of time in which anything can be learned is one period. What subject matter can be learned in-depth in an hour? What kind of jobs can people learn to perform in an hour?

Showing up. In urban schools there is a tacit working agreement between students and teachers that I refer to as "The Deal". If a student does not disrupt the class, the teacher in return, ignores the fact that the student does not turn in any work. The operating norm is, "If you don't bother me I won't bother you. Simple attendance is, thus, transformed into a virtue. Just being there is all that matters. Work is not expected—only the absence of negative behavior.

Teachers purchase this peace with a grade of D minus. The student's logic is, "If I never showed up I would get an F, but I showed up and I deserve something for it." But passing students simply for being there systematically teaches them that mere existence merits a reward. They never learn that attendance is a necessary but not sufficient condition for being rewarded. By rewarding inaction, lack of involvement and detachment, urban schools promulgate the dangerous myth that one can expect to be rewarded for merely showing up and not causing trouble. The standard that is set for doing "satisfactory" work is merely showing up. What jobs can be performed by just showing up?

Make me. Urban schools are authoritarian settings in which control is the ultimate criterion for judging success. Many more principals are removed because their buildings lack sufficient controls than because their students are failing to learn. The need to create a safe school environment in an unsafe neighborhood is, of course, understandable and desirable. But the authoritarianism used to maintain a safe building is typically extended to the curriculum and the teaching-learning process as well. The students see endless rules, a prescribed curriculum and the pedagogy of poverty. In an overly directive climate it is inevitable that students come to believe that school staff decide everything and that school is essentially "their deal not ours". This climate effectively teaches students that it is the teachers' responsibility to make students learn.

By allowing and rewarding students for being passive witnesses, urban schools support students' perceptions that all relationships are essentially authoritarian. As urban youngsters see the world, they are compelled to go to school while teachers are paid to be there. Therefore, it is the teachers' job to make them learn. Every school policy and decision that is arrived at without involving students—and that means virtually all of them—supports the perception that principals and teachers rather than students, are the school constituency that must be held accountable for learning. In arriving at this view, students are being logical. After all, in an authoritarian, top-down system that grants no voice to those at the bottom, why should the individuals who are "being done to" be held accountable? What jobs can be performed without the employees feeling any sense of accountability?

Excuses. Of all the unemployment values that urban schools teach, they teach this one best! Students are taught to believe that they can be late or absent as often as they have a good excuse. What has been taught in their

UNEMPLOYMENT TRAINING: THE IDEOLOGY OF NON-WORK LEARNED IN URBAN SCHOOLS

absence is of no consequence to them since they are not held accountable for knowing anything they missed if they had a good excuse. What matters is the quality of the excuse and with good excuses, there is no limit to the number of times a student can be absent or late and still be "passing". The value taught is, "If it's not your fault that you are absent, then it's as good as being there. And "being there" passes.

In a survey I conducted in an urban middle school, students were asked the question, "How many times can you be absent (or late) in a month and hold a regular job?" Over half of the students responded that they could be absent or late as often as they had a good excuse.

In direct observations in schools and in a half century of interactions with urban teachers, it is clear to me that youngsters feel zero responsibility for making up missed schoolwork—or for even finding out what they missed. Students are fixated with only the quality of their excuses. When asked directly, "How do you learn what you missed?" students are unable to respond because they do not believe they have to make up anything they missed. A few reply, "Review is what teachers do." What jobs can be held by people who believe that they can be late or absent as frequently as they have a good excuse?

Non-cooperation. When urban youth have differences with their peers, they typically react with threats or force. Almost any body language or verbal interaction may escalate violence. The value that students bring to school is, "Might makes right." Some urban schools seek to teach non-violent options and peer mediation. They also employ negative reinforcement to cut down on overly aggressive behavior. But despite the great frequency of detentions, suspensions and expulsions, the most frequent school response to students' interpersonal problems is to separate the potential combatants. It is easier, and therefore, most common for administrators, teachers and safety aides to simply separate disputing students than it is to teach them to get along. Students become conditioned to expect that they will be separated, and thus, do not try to learn new ways of improving communication with rivals. This constant segregation as a "solution" to violence prevents students from ever practicing any form of peaceful co-existence.

63

STAR TEACHERS

A second reason the street values of power and control are reinforced in school is that school staff cannot protect students outside of school. Students and their parents believe that students must learn to take care of their own "business".The problem is exacerbated by the fact that even in school where educators do control the environment, there is no systematic training in using alternatives to violence. Instead educators take the easy way out by pretending that violent behavior among urban youngsters cannot be reversed; therefore, the simplest strategy—i.e. separating potential combatants—is the best one. By implementing this strategy consistently for thirteen years, urban schools solidly reinforce in their students the myth that cooperative behavior is unnecessary. Those who believe that people should never have to work with anyone one they don't like will never be able to function in any work situation.

Respect. The naïve or the uninitiated might assume that the schools teach students to respect those who know a lot, those who can learn a lot, or those who at least try hard. But these values carry little weight with urban students. Indeed, those who try hard and demonstrate initiative are perceived negatively as to a dying to authority. Power is the basis upon which students give or receive respect. The critical question is, "Who can do what to whom?" Respect accrues to those with the power to hurt.

In response to the question, "When is it okay to hit people?" urban school students provide a bizarre list of what constitutes being "dissed" including, "he talked funny" and "he looked at me crazy." Clearly, urban youngsters believe that words or glances that they perceive as provocative require a physical response, which can range from hitting to killing.

The issue is not students' street values, per se, but the ways in which schools reinforce these values rather than teach alternatives. The concept that one "earns" respect by doing good deeds is almost unheard of among urban youngsters. They extend respect (except for sports figures and rock stars) to those with the power to inflict physical harm.

Schools have no real power to physically hurt students once they reach the age or stature when parents can no longer apply physical punishment. As children become adolescents, teachers are less able to send negative reports

64

to parents who will then inflict physical punishment. At they reach physical maturity, students using the power criterion as a standard for awarding respect see no reason to respect school staff.

The only reasonable option for the schools is to neither condone nor use power alone to control students. Admittedly this will be difficult (especially in the twenty-two states where corporal punishment is still legal), but continuing current school policies merely teaches youth that schools are no different from the street—just less effective in the use of power. What sort of jobs can people hold if they believe that they only need to respect those who can hurt them?

Authority. Students' responses to school authority are influenced by their belief that institutions of all kinds are out to get them. The criminal justice system, the welfare system, the health care system and the housing authority are just a few of the institutions with which families in poverty must interact repeatedly. Because urban schools relate to students and their families in the same impersonal, controlling, legalistic ways as these other institutions, students and their families perceive the schools as just another institution with which they must contend.

Urban schools begin teaching students a dysfunctional way of relating to authority in kindergarten. Young children are readily controlled by authoritarian, directive teaching and simple rewards. As children mature, however, they come to realize that school authorities lack any real power to make them comply. Relating to school authorities then becomes a game. Since students neither identify with the school nor feel ownership of the rules and regulations, the goal of the game is to make school authorities look bad, or stupid, or unable to enforce compliance. The students win this game while in school, but as graduates they lose. It is hard to hold any job, even an unskilled one, if the employee's goal is to demonstrate that the employer is unable to enforce complete authority and absolute compliance.

Peers. There's nothing new about the strong influence that peers have always exerted on adolescent behavior. What's different today is the nature of the street values that students bring to school. Given those values, behavior that adults see as bad or irrational is often quite sensible. When one lives in a violent neighborhood, for example, does it make sense to join a group that offers protection?

Peer groups are extremely influential in teaching students how to behave in school. Their teachings, however, tend to focus on what not to do: don't carry books, don't do homework, don't take responsibility, don't prepare for classes, and don't remember things. The central message to students in middle and high school is, "Don't participate. Just show up and watch them try to get you to do stuff." The public, the media and educational experts focus on those students who act out and challenge school authority in overtly aggressive ways, but they ignore the significantly greater number of urban youngsters whose negative behavior is a more powerful passive resistance. What does thirteen years of practice at being part of a peer group playing "try and make me" portend for a graduate's ability to function in the world of work?

Messing up. Urban students strongly believe that no matter how often one does something wrong or neglects to perform an expected behavior, s/he deserves another chance. Students deem the failure to provide an endless number of additional chances as "unfair"—and in their view, no action on their part warrants not getting another chance. The schools effectively teach that there are never final consequences for one's behavior only endless chances.

Urban schools inculcate and pander to this belief that nothing students can do is serious enough to prevent getting another chance. The epitome of this teaching occurs when students are transferred from one school to another so that the particular schools can claim they have zero suspensions or dropouts. Many districts establish special alternative schools in which they warehouse "troublemakers". Typically these students become ghosts; they are carried on the attendance rolls of the district for the purpose of securing state aid but have, in effect, disappeared. Every major urban district has thousands of such ghosts; some have tens of thousands. If all the ghosts were to show up and actually attend, no urban district would be able to cope with their number without floating a bond issue to build additional schools.

In short, urban schools accept the street value that their job is to compel student learning, rather than doing everything possible to encourage, interest, motivate and make students want to learn. Once the schools accept this "make me" challenge it leads to the inevitable cycle of escalating punishments to force compliance.

In this climate the lessons learned by "successful" students are even more devastating than those learned by dropouts. After thirteen years of never completing assignments or any sustained learning activities and yet always getting another chance, the lesson learned is that it's okay to do whatever one pleases. Will graduates be able to function in the world of work if they have been carefully taught that "fairness" means always getting another chance regardless of how serious the mistake or how often it is committed?

Explaining success. When urban youngsters are asked to explain the cause of success in school they mention several factors, including ability, luck and connections. The factor they are least likely to cite is effort. The reason for this is that students believe it is not cool to put a lot of effort into school activities. If one tries hard and fails, it shows that one is stupid. If one tries hard and succeeds it shows that one is not as intelligent as the individual who expends no effort and still manages to pass. Urban students aspire to be perfect with no effort or preparation at all.

Teachers frequently misinterpret this situation and assume that because students refuse or actually resist being helped that they do not want to learn. Students' resistance to teachers' help is especially strong when help is offered in front of peers. But how much can students learn if they believe they are not supposed to make mistakes in front of peers? How much can students learn if they pretend (or really believe) that being smart means you simply know things without having to expend any effort studying or practicing?

Schools play into and support these student behaviors and foster this value. Teachers, who do not actively involve students in challenging, thoughtful activities, encourage students to see effort as a sign of inadequacy. Schools that emphasize correct answers in place of substantial thinking miss many opportunities to teach students that the path to achievement and success is sustained effort. Thomas Edison once said, "The difference between coal and diamonds is that diamonds stayed on the job longer. What does believing that one can be successful without sustained effort portend for a career in any field?

Relevance. It is incumbent on teachers to help students see the connections between their life experiences and the content to be learned. But this does not mean limiting the curriculum to the experiences of the students. The very purpose of education is to push students beyond their present understandings—to open their minds and imaginations to the universe of great ideas past, present and future. To do anything less is to lower expectations and standards. Making content relevant by limiting it to students' current life experiences is not meeting students' needs but pandering to ignorance.

Experiencing things directly is powerful but just one way of knowing—a starting point for understanding the world. Education provides other ways of knowing: learning from the experiences and ideas of others, from the findings of research, from theories of how things work, from intuition, from the arts and humanities. If one is limited to learning only that which is directly experienced, one is a hostage, not a beneficiary of personal experience. The criterion of immediacy should not be used to limit learning. Students will live out their lives under conditions yet to be imagined. If students plan their future in terms of only the jobs they see around them in their neighborhoods, they will be using their experiences to limit their aspirations in the world of work. In order for students to have access and opportunity to careers of value they must be led to see opportunities that are beyond those in their immediate experience.

Purpose. The learning of skills to an advanced and useful degree is frequently not fun. Leaning concepts can also be hard work. In many cases, attaining valuable knowledge can be genuine drudgery. But the converse is not true: when school work is drudgery it is not evidence that useful learning is occurring.

Urban students not only believe that a good teacher is one who can make them learn but that s/he can always make learning fun. Naturally, teachers should make every effort to stimulate and engage their students. But fun cannot be the ultimate standard for judging teachers' effectiveness. Students must often learn difficult and complex things. Many of these things require memorization, intense concentration and fatiguing repetitions. Such learning is seldom fun.

If schools accede to and support the notion that good learning is always fun what are they teaching students about the world of work? Should we be teaching students that their future employers have an obligation to make their jobs fun?

Staying on task. Urban schools are places where students come and go all day. Urban schools have an average of 125 interruptions every week. It is not unusual for students to stay on task for ten minutes in any given hour. Textbook companies and curriculum reformers are constantly dismayed by this reality. When they sell their materials and programs to schools they assure the schools that all students will learn X amount in Y time. But an hour of school time is never an hour of learning time. As many insightful observers of life in urban schools have pointed out, it is incredibly naïve to believe that learning subject matter is the main activity occurring in urban schools. How does changing activities every 45 minutes prepare students for holding a job? How does staying on task for only a few minutes out of every hour prepare them for jobs where they will be expected to work continuously on tasks that extend eight or more hours, day in and day out?

Ignorance of rules. Students know that the best way to circumvent the rules is to not know them. Urban schools do not hold the uninformed responsible. This practice plays right into students' hands. Lists of school rules are sent home. Parents are asked to sign statements that they have read them. But students who don't learn a rule the first time are simply taught it again. This makes classroom and school rules exactly like other school content—"something the teacher is responsible for making me learn." What does this approach to following rules portend for students' future performance in the workplace?

The fourteen parts of the urban students' ideology outlined above interact in ways that teach youngsters that they have no stake in the process of schooling. Adults assume the students perceive of themselves as learners. Not so! The students show up because they have to, because they need someplace to go everyday, because they need the approval of their peers and to have lunch. As early as third grade many students are turned off. By middle school most believe that schooling is irrelevant to their present and future lives.

Many schools encourage students to disconnect. In countless ways urban schools communicate the message that students are not essential to what is going on. Indeed, one of the major differences between star teachers and quitter/failure teachers is that star teachers convince their students that they are essential and needed: "We couldn't do what we have to do in this classroom without your total participation." Teachers who fail in urban settings communicate the reverse: "This is my class. If you don't shape up you're out of here."

If students are taught that the success of the total operation is not dependent on their participation, what happens to them when they become workers? Can they become assets in the workplace if they believe that the success of the total organization has nothing to do with them?

Implications for Future Workers

"Successful graduates" infected as most are by this ideology of non-work are unlikely to land a job and keep it—unless the following conditions apply.

- There is no screening process or requirements for getting the job beyond showing up.
- There is no previous training required. Whatever the job involves can be explained in a few minutes—certainly less than forty-five minutes.
- There is a boss who will watch the workers at all times to make sure they work.
- The boss will always be present.
- The boss is responsible for what the workers do.
- The workers will be able to be "off-task" as frequently as they please and still keep their jobs.
- A worker may be late or absent as frequently as s/he has a good excuse.
- There is never any need to make up any time or any work after being absent.
- The worker won't have to work with or talk to anyone s/he doesn't like.

- The worker doesn't have to listen to anyone but the boss.
- There is nothing to prepare in order to come to work.
- There is nothing to do related to the job after quitting time.
- Pay is based on the time spent at work, never on what is accomplished.
- The job never changes.
- Pay raises are based on length of time on the job.
- The worker need not demonstrate respect for anyone who lacks the power to hurt him/her.
- If the work gets messed up it is the boss' problem.
- If the business fails it is not the worker's problem.
- No matter how many mistakes the worker makes, s/he will always be given another chance.
- The work will always be fun.
- There's no need to follow any rules of the workplace unless the boss can prove the rules were directly explained to you personally.
- There's no need to actually work, i.e. stay on task, for more than a few minutes each hour.

Any job that could actually meet these twenty-two conditions would have certain other characteristics as well. It would have to involve many workers all doing the very same tasks so that an individual's absences would not matter. It would also likely be a job that did not involve great time pressures or deadlines since workers would not always be on-task. It could not be a job in which the quality of the work was a primary concern. It would probably be a menial job without any career path since no previous training or experience is required. It could not be a job in which the success of the organization is tied to the worker's effort. Given these limitations, which derive directly from the ideology of nonwork learned in urban schools, what kind of jobs could graduates get and actually perform? Even a part-time job putting laundry into washing machines in the basement of a hotel would require a greater work ethic than is reflected in the twenty-two beliefs comprising this ideology.

What Can Be Done?

Before this situation can be transformed, urban educators must recognize and admit that they are effectively teaching this non-work ideology to both dropouts and graduates. They will then have to reexamine every school policy and teachers' daily practices to identify all the ways in which this ideology is taught everyday. After such a careful self-examination the administrators, faculty and staff of each school will need to plan alternative strategies to those currently rewarding the behaviors of non-work. Such a careful reexamination may take some time. Cleansing the school of debilitating traditions is not a simple task.

What is currently taking place in urban schools is not teaching and learning. It is a battle between teachers and students over who is socializing who. Are school values trumping street values or vice versa? Will urban educators be able to socialize their students for the world of work or will students continue to socialize the educators to practice street values in the schools? Currently it is not a contest. The street values of the students are clearly the dominant force in how urban schools operate. The way in which the curriculum is offered in urban schools and even more, the rules governing the daily life of the school support the non-work ideology of the street not the values that lead to success and achievement in the larger society. The solution is for urban educators to immediately stop doing all the things that so effectively reward and reinforce the ideology of non-work and substitute rewards for students who expend effort, persist at learning higher order skills, work cooperatively and relate to each other in non-authoritarian ways. Before school cultures can be transformed, those who work in them must first understand how the students shape the teachers behavior by rewarding them with compliance. This is a very powerful reward because it leads teachers and administrators to believe they are in charge when in reality it is the students who decide the conditions with which they will comply. Until teachers and administrators understand the process by which students are controlling the situation, the schools will continue to foster an ideology and behaviors which are antithetic to success in the world of work.

Part Three: Star Teachers: Their Ideology and Behaviors

Chapter X
The Research Base of Star Teacher Functions

Previous Studies

During the 1930's and 1940's, A.S.Barr and his students at the University of Wisconsin conducted, literally, hundreds of studies, mostly masters and doctoral theses, on "What makes a good teacher?" They studied this question over and over with teachers at every grade level and in every subject matter. They identified hundreds of personal, professional and social characteristics of teachers. These studies were generic in the sense that they assumed a good teacher was universally good with all students regardless of their economic level or ethnic background. Identifying "good" teachers was done by aggregating various observers' opinions about them rather than by connecting teacher attributes to student learning. When Barr retired and reviewed his career he concluded that his contributions had still not identified what a universally good teacher was. Barr also questioned whether there were universal qualities of teacher goodness which could predict success in teaching all grades and content areas to all children and youth.

In the 1950's and 1960's, David G. Ryans did connect student outcomes with what he called X, Y or Z teacher personality patterns. The X pattern was described as creative, dynamic and outgoing. The Y pattern was described as business-like and well organized. The Z pattern was described as dull, remote and aloof. In Ryan's sample (i.e. white, middle class suburban and small town children and youth) the Y pattern seemed to correlate with the greatest student achievement. While the Y teachers seemed to have the greatest impact, Ryans never studied the process of how best to select and prepare teachers with such characteristics.

STAR TEACHERS

Psychological vs. Situational Predictors

During this period I began to examine studies of how professionals were prepared in fields other than teaching. There seemed to be a clear consensus on the psychological approach. This approach assumes that the variables which are most powerful in predicting and controlling the professional's behavior after training exist in the personality make-up of the individual being trained; that is, in every profession there is a psychological profile of who will be successful in practicing that particular profession with all clients in all settings.

This line of research derived directly from E.L. Thorndike who laid out a detailed set of predictions based on his test of intelligence. Those with a particular I.Q. score would be suitable for a specific job, e.g. an individual with a score of 85 could be successful as a shoe salesman but not the store manager. Someone with an IQ score of 90 was suited to be a bank teller but not a loan officer and so forth. As Thorndike's students continued his work they developed not only IQ tests but psychological profiles which predicted an individual's suitability for every job and profession. This approach is still widely used today in many private companies and by governmental agencies which test job seekers to determine their psychological profiles. From salespeople to astronauts it is now commonly accepted that everyone has a psychological profile which is a valid indicator for predicting that individual's appropriateness for performing a specific job. If possessed of the "right" personal qualities it is presumed that the individual practitioner will be successful performing that job with clients, in all settings, under any conditions of work.

In opposition to this approach sociologists and social scientists in other disciplines have analyzed the various professions and argued that the most powerful variables which control and predict professional behavior are to be found in the situations and conditions in which individuals work and not in the personalities or assumed intelligence of the practitioners. What does emphasizing the demands of the setting rather than the personality of the individual mean for how professionals should be selected and trained? If the psychological approach is valid, then a good teacher is a good teacher everywhere with everyone. If the sociological approach is valid and the conditions of work and the particular clients control much of the practitioner's behavior, then different teachers must be selected and trained to serve different clients in different settings. Those who believe that the nature of the setting and the clients are more likely to control the behavior of the practitioner, than the nature of the professional's personality profile frequently analyze a particular job in terms of the specific behaviors that must be performed. They compile the specific tasks and functions that must be demonstrated by professionals in a particular setting. The training models they develop are based on the professional behaviors required to function effectively in a particular time and place. Rather than seek individuals with the personality profile to make them successful everywhere, they select and train the most appropriate individuals for particular situations.

The Mid-Range Functions

Robert K. Merton argued that both of these approaches were extremes and dysfunctional guidelines for action. It is not possible to generalize from teachers' personality profiles how they will behave in future with all types of children in all kinds of school situations. Having a psychological profile that a teacher is shy or aggressive, introverted or extroverted, warm or business-like, does not enable us to predict that teacher's effectiveness in all schools. Unfortunately, many school districts buy into this approach and still use psychological profiles as they seek to hire the universally good teacher. This widespread practice contributes to the churn of teachers; that is, the coming and going of quitters and failures all of whom have passed these psychological profile tests but are not able to cope with the demands of actually teaching diverse children in poverty in specific schools in failing urban school districts. At the other extreme, using the situational model and breaking down professional practice into hundreds of discrete behaviors which must be performed in a particular setting does not enable us to identify and prepare professionals who will perform all those tasks effectively. For example, the State of Wisconsin has summarized the research on teaching and identified "the" 127 behaviors of effective teachers. The list is useless because it does not rank these behaviors in terms of importance. Neither can it tell the practitioner when to perform which task for how long. A good example of the inadequacy of using only the behavioral approach is the case of air line attendants. When asked their most important function they respond, "saving lives in an emergency." Many, however, work their entire careers without ever once saving anyone's life. Can a job's most important function be a behavior that is never performed? An examination of only behaviors cannot adequately explain what a practitioner actually does.

To resolve this dilemma Merton came up with the concept of "mid-range functions". "Mid-range functions" are based on the assumption that the practice of any profession is both a reflection of the practitioners' predispositions and the nature of the performance demands in particular settings. Merton also discovered that the most powerful predictor of professional behavior is not a personality profile but an individual's ideology. And the most critical behaviors to be performed are not endless lists of discrete tasks but functions which involve the performance of multiple tasks grouped together into more general functions. These functions are clusters, chunks or groups of behaviors. It is likely that there are fewer than ten mid-range functions performed by successful practitioners in any profession. An ideology appropriate to serving particular clients in specific situations must undergird and provide the foundation for performing these functions. Rather than a universal personality profile, which has no predictive validity, the professional's ideology is a set of beliefs and commitments which control, shape and predict his/her future behavior. In teaching, the practitioners' ideology is reflected in the explanations they give themselves regarding the purpose of schools, the role of the teacher, the causes of the achievement gap and the factors that cause diverse children in urban poverty to be successful in poor schools. In sum, mid-range functions are behavioral clusters which are relatively small in number and which are performed by practitioners with a particular ideology under specific conditions of work. Rather than search for individuals who are assumed to be universally competent, the need is to select individuals who will perform mid-range functions with particular clients in particular school settings. This approach explains and helps us understand how there can be effective teachers in advantaged school settings who would be quitters and failures in urban school districts serving diverse students in poverty.

At this time I was also influenced by the work of J. S. Becker whose study The Boys in White analyzed what makes medical interns effective.

Becker found that the real training of medical doctors did not occur until after graduation when they were placed in hospitals as interns and actually required to function in the role of responsible, accountable doctors treating real live patients. The interns in this study made it clear that the extensive, agreed-upon body of knowledge they had learned was necessary background but hadn't really prepared them for their work as interns in emergency rooms. They believed they really learned to be doctors by functioning on-the-job with the help of mentors in a particular hospital setting serving specific clients. I realized this process of learning on-the-job as an accountable intern was even more valid for teachers because the teacher's research base has many fewer, less valid studies and nothing remotely resembling an agreed-upon knowledge base. What teachers learn in one school of education is not the same (except for course titles) as what they learn in another. And most of what they learn in any university program of teacher education is essentially faculty folk wisdom and advocacies, not an agreed-upon, solid research base explaining what causes diverse constituencies of children and youth in poverty to learn in failing school districts. Becker's work led me to examine how professionals are prepared in several professions. In every case the responses of the neophyte practitioners were the same. They claimed to learn the essentials of their practice after graduation by working on-the-job with real clients. I came to realize that this was even more true in the case of teacher education. Teacher preparation for the real world does not and cannot occur in university settings but in situ. Like the interns in any profession, the actual training occurs after graduation during the first year (internship) of responsible, accountable performance on-the-job, in a particular setting with the help of mentors. The nature of the setting, the community, the school and the particular students all combine in ways that make learning to teach like learning any profession. The only way one can learn to be responsible and accountable is by actually being responsible and accountable to particular clients in a particular setting.

The Fable of the "Best and the Brightest"

Between 1958 and 1962, while a doctoral student in Teachers College, Columbia University, I had the opportunity to serve as a supervisor of student teachers and the evaluator of a fifth year program of teacher preparation. The students in this masters/certification program were all young women under twenty-five who were recent liberal arts graduates from Barnard, Radcliff, Swarthmore, Vassar, Smith, Mt. Holyoke, Bennington, Sarah Lawrence and similar elite institutions. These students were all highly educated women with first rate accomplishments in the liberal arts from some of America's best colleges. During the course of their full-time, year long program they completed forty credits in education with very prestigious teacher educators at T.C. Columbia. For the population completing this program, there could be no question that they knew both subject matter content and pedagogy at levels much higher than teacher education graduates from typical schools of education. In terms of research this was an ideal group to test the shibboleth that the most appropriate pool from which to draw teachers for diverse children in urban poverty is to tap "the best and brightest" to become their teachers.

As part of their training we placed these students into New York City public schools in Harlem neighborhoods serving diverse children in urban poverty. The cultural divide between these advantaged preservice teachers and the disadvantaged children and youth they were attempting to teach was as wide a gulf as could possibly be imagined. We assessed these beginning teachers with attitude tests, value scales and personality inventories, including the Lorge Thorndike Test of Intelligence, the Minnesota Multiphasic Personality Inventory, the Minnesota Teacher Attitude Inventory, Allport's Test of Social Distance, Torrence's Test of Creativity, and Ryan's test of Effective Teacher Characteristics. The scores on none of these tests correlated with or predicted their ability to establish rapport and relate to the children they were trying to teach. Teachers' test scores also did not correlate with their students' achievement. Another way to state these findings is that teacher candidates scoring high or positive on tests of intelligence, personality, social values, teacher attitudes, characteristics and creativity were no more likely to perform well with diverse students in poverty than those who scored low on these assessments. Indeed, there was actually a low negative correlation between scores on these assessments and the ability of the teacher candidates to relate and sustain positive interactions with the children. The reason for this lack of predictive validity is that high scores on these assessments do not identify teacher candidates who want to teach diverse, low-income children. These tests also do not identify the kind of individuals the children want for their teachers. In the course of these four years approximately 124 of these "best and brightest" women completed the program. As with no other study in preservice teacher education, this year-long study was replicated four times and yielded the same results in each iteration.

Upon completion of the program only eighteen of the 124 graduates actually took teaching positions and these were in suburban and private schools. None remained in teaching longer then two years. None sought positions in New York City. All moved on to other careers and raising families. In effect, the traditional criteria used to determine "the best and the brightest" (i.e. high college grades, graduation from first rate liberal arts colleges, advanced knowledge of subject matter and professional content, and high scores on assessments of what experts regard as the "right" personality profile, actually identified individuals who would be most likely to pass through the profession not stay in it. The findings of these studies are unequivocal. The criteria used to identify "the best and the brightest" actually identify failure/quitter teachers of diverse children in poverty. Yet, this shibboleth remains a popular advocacy even after forty-five years of evidence to the contrary.

The most important findings of these studies, however, dealt with the candidates' effectiveness in the Harlem schools. On the basis of their demonstrated performance as evaluated by multiple observers, they readily divided themselves into three groups: about ten percent were Stars who were truly great in their ability to relate to diverse students in poverty and could get their students to demonstrate learning; about thirty percent could relate to some of the students some of the time but actually taught very little; and about sixty percent could not relate to or teach the children very much of anything. The major finding of these studies was that only one in ten individuals under twenty-five years of age, with advanced knowledge of content and pedagogy relate well to diverse children in poverty and that none would seek to teach in poverty schools...or stay in teaching anywhere for longer than two years, and that the attributes used in traditional programs of teacher education to predict success and staying power actually predict failures and quitters.

Star Teachers

The Truly Best and Brightest

The search for meaning is the primary attraction of teaching to mature adults. There is also a set of background factors which do predict who will be effective and remain in schools serving diverse students in poverty. Many who have the potential to become effective teachers will not have all of these attributes, but the population of mature adults who become effective and remain in these classrooms tend to have many of the following characteristics:

- they are over age thirty,
- they live in or were raised in a metropolitan area,
- they have attended schools in a metropolitan area as a child or youth,
- they are parents or have had life experiences which involved extensive relationships with children,
- they are African American, Latino, members of a minority group, or from a working class white family,
- they earned a bachelors degree from other than a highly selective or elitist college; many started in community colleges,
- they majored in a field other than education as an undergraduate,
- they have had extensive and varied work experiences before seeking to become teachers,
- they are part of a family/church/ethnic community in which teaching is still regarded as a fairly high-status career,
- they have experienced a period of living in poverty or have the capacity to empathize with the challenges of living in poverty,
- they have had out-of-school experiences with children of diverse backgrounds,
- they may have had military experience but not as an officer,
- they live in the city or would have no objection to moving into the city to meet a residency requirement,
- they have engaged in paid or volunteer activities with diverse children in poverty,
- they can multitask and do several things simultaneously and quickly for extended periods, such as parenting and working part time jobs.

These attributes do not guarantee success as an urban teacher; they raise the probability that individuals with these attributes will succeed and remain. The reverse of these attributes describes a pool of people who are unlikely to remain in poverty schools. Unfortunately, many districts still recruit and hire only the traditional pool: i.e. middle class, white, monolingual, late adolescent females who graduated from suburban, small town and parochial schools, who were full-time undergraduate majors in education, with little or no work or life experiences, without families or child-rearing experience, and who lack commitment to or roots in a particular urban area. Again, all of these characteristics are not required but having a cluster of them is typical of individuals who succeed and stay in urban schools. These fifteen attributes and not undergraduate GPA, describe "the best and the brightest" population for teaching diverse students in poverty.

While teaching will remain a predominantly female career, more mature males can and should be recruited and prepared. As with females, the most powerful predictor is age; as more mature males are recruited, the numbers who succeed and remain increases substantially. In addition to the characteristics outlined above the males who succeed with diverse children in poverty are characterized by nine additional attributes. They are willing and able to:

- work in feminine institutions where procedures and human relationships with other adults are of greater importance than outcomes,
- take directions and accept evaluations from female principals and female supervisors
- implement criticism not stated as direct orders but as "suggestions" or "concerns",
- spend a good part of every day encouraging and nurturing children and youth as well as teaching them,
- interact positively with mothers and female care-givers,
- maintain class control by motivating and relating to children rather than by trying to dominate them,
- regard children's misbehavior as a professional problem to be resolved rather than a threat to their authority or manliness,
- make personal sacrifices of time and energy to meet student's needs,
- multi-task and perform several functions simultaneously.

STAR TEACHERS

Men with all or most of these attributes succeed as urban teachers. They are men who are able to understand and overcome the way males are typically socialized in our society. In all teacher education programs a higher percentage of males than females quit or fail, but by selecting men who have the nine additional attributes cited above, the programs I have developed have produced as many as one-third male graduates who prove to be effective and who stay in teaching.

Research Based Guidelines of Urban Teacher Preparation

As a result of these studies I came to seven beliefs about teacher preparation which I decided were worth acting on and researching further.

1. The typical criteria used by colleges and universities to select teacher candidates, and the assessment tests used by state departments of education to license teachers, have no predictive validity. If used as screening and selection devices they are more likely to identify failure/quitter teachers than effective ones. Similarly, the psychological profiles still used by school districts to hire teachers correlate negatively with subsequent teacher performance and staying power.
2. Teacher education is not a generic process which can prepare universally competent practitioners. The preparation of teachers for diverse children in poverty requires recruiting new populations of teacher candidates prepared in specific school settings for communities with particular client groups.
3. Mature college graduates from all fields of study, who have had work and life experiences, are ten times more likely to be successful in teaching diverse children in poverty than young undergraduates who majored in education.
4. Selection is more important than training. It is easier and wiser to select individuals who share the predispositions of effective, star teachers succeeding in urban schools than to admit individuals into training programs without this ideology and hope that education courses and student teaching will somehow transform their value systems.
5. Teacher training actually occurs in real schools as candidates function in the role of responsible teachers of record, not in university based

teacher training programs where candidates function in the role of university students unaccountable for children's learning and free of the negative conditions under which teachers in failing urban school districts must work. Training must occur in the real world not in the best of all non-existent ones.

6. Typical college faculty in schools of education do not have the experiential basis required for preparing candidates to teach diverse children in urban poverty schools because they have not done it themselves. The most appropriate teacher education faculty, are classroom teachers who have demonstrated their effectiveness with diverse children and youth in poverty for sustained periods who then serve as on-the-job mentors.

7. Recommending individuals for teacher licenses should occur at the end of an intern ear in which candidates have served as accountable teachers of record and require that candidates provide evidence of satisfactory increases in their students' learning.

The Lessons of the National Teacher Corps

In 1962, I incorporated the seven lessons cited above into a fifth year intern program at the University of Wisconsin Milwaukee. At that time $75 per year covered the full cost of a teacher's health insurance. The Milwaukee Public Schools agreed to a pattern in which they would employ two teacher interns working half time for half pay to cover one teacher's workload. The interns served as fully responsible teachers of record and learned to teach on-the-job supported by on-site mentors. Training a pair of interns on-the-job in this way only cost the schools $75 and enabled the system to hire new teachers who already had demonstrated effectiveness with diverse children in poverty. In place of sixty credits of education courses (or thirty for secondary students), interns took one weekly course focused on helping them solve their day-to-day classroom problems and apply research-based strategies of instruction. The second year the interns each carried a full teaching load. This not only solved the urban district's teacher shortage but provided them with a large pool of mature college graduates as new teachers…those whom we assumed would stay in teaching. In 1963, Senator Nelson and Senator Kennedy adopted my model and it became the National Teacher Corps. Between 1963 and 1972, approximately 100,000 college graduates from fields other than education participated in internship programs in poverty schools all over America. Corpsmen were certified after one year of teaching as responsible teachers of record. Using federal grants, eighty-two colleges and universities cooperated with school districts in developing new ways to prepare teachers on-the-job with the help of classroom teachers serving as mentors. This was the largest, longest research demonstration project ever undertaken in teacher education.

While the Teacher Corps greatly enhanced my reputation it was a notable failure. I was, however, able to study it in-depth and learn what works and what doesn't in securing teachers for the real world. After the federal support was discontinued all eighty-two colleges and universities that had participated in the program dropped it and returned to preparing late adolescents (18-22 year olds) in traditional undergraduate programs. If one flips a coin eighty-two times and gets only tails it is clear that there are factors operating other than chance. Once the federal monies stopped, the participating colleges and universities lost their "passionate commitment" to getting teachers for children in poverty. The basic lesson which should have been learned from this grand experiment and one which is still generally ignored, is that systemic institutional change in schools of education (or in higher education generally) is not accomplished with grant funds. Second, over ninety percent of the corpsmen were middle-class whites who remained as classroom teachers for three years or less. The few who stayed in education moved "upward" into administration or central offices. Third, after 1973, new patterns of recruiting and preparing teachers were not adopted; they regressed back to offering only traditional programs. More mature, urban-oriented adults were not widely recruited again until the shortages of the 1990's. Fourth, there was not a general acceptance of intern programs or alternative certification as the best ways to prepare teachers for diverse children in poverty in failing school districts. Indeed, schools of education have demonstrated resistance and hostility to the threat of on-the-job programs. Fifth, there was no increase in the diversity of the teaching force. In sum, neither the schools nor the universities were changed in any important ways by having participated in the National Teacher Corps. These findings are well documented in Ron Corwin's book, The National Teacher Corps as an Educational Change Strategy.

THE RESEARCH BASE OF STAR TEACHER FUNCTIONS

Obviously, training teachers while they serve as the responsible teachers of record requires protecting children and youth from poor teachers. In the intern model it is necessary to make certain that the teachers identified can learn on-the-job while not wasting the time of the children and youth they are teaching. The first selection study I conducted, therefore, compared the learning of children in the rooms of interns with the achievement of children in the rooms of veteran teachers prepared in traditional programs of teacher education. The results indicated that children in the rooms of interns (selected on the basis of stars teachers' predispositions) achieved at the same level as children in the rooms of veteran teachers in the same school settings. In the subsequent forty-five years all my replications of this comparison between interns selected with the Star Urban Teacher Interview and veteran teachers have indicated that children's achievement has been the same or higher in the rooms of the interns. The last replication was in 2003, in the Milwaukee Public Schools. Further, mature interns remained in teaching while half of the traditional college-age youth quit or failed in five years or less. To have interns learning on-the-job as first year teachers do as well (as measured by student achievement) as veteran teachers, is a highly significant finding. Consider the time and resources that are saved by not taking traditional teacher education curricula. Consider also the fact that more mature, diverse populations with work and life experiences are brought into teaching through such models. The critical point is the fact that mature adults who are successful and remain teaching diverse children in poverty are willingly recruited into teaching if they can function in the role of responsible, fully paid teachers of record. They are not willing to become teachers if they have to function in the role of college students in schools of education.

In order to protect children and identify teachers who would be successful and stay in teaching, it was necessary to develop a selection process with predictive validity. Between 1963 and 1972, my colleagues and I conducted approximately 3,000 interviews to determine if the predispositions we isolated as characteristic of star teachers in urban schools could be identified in an interview. The process I followed was to first identify the functions that distinguished stars from quitter/failures. Then to develop interview questions which assessed these functions. The responses of star teachers became the best answers to the questions and the responses of the quitter/failures the unacceptable responses. Star teachers were identified by seven constituencies:

other teachers, students, parents, principals, central office supervisors, college faculty and themselves. If all agreed that this was "one of the best teachers in the school" we examined the test scores of their students in reading and math for elementary teachers and in the particular subject areas for middle and high school teachers. In addition to the opinions of the various constituencies and test scores we used a third criterion. Two observers visited the classrooms of the teachers nominated as stars. Using the observation schedule of Marie Hughes, which has the most solid research base supporting its assessment categories, the nominees' teaching were directly observed and evaluated. Of the 118 veteran teachers studied in the first year, 17 were identified as stars and 48 as failure quitters. Over the nine year period the number of stars averaged 10% and the number of quitter/failures 50%. These proportions have remained characteristic of the 120 largest urban school districts over the last forty-five years.

The next step was for teams of two to interview each of these teachers regarding their classroom practices to determine the "mid-range functions" they saw themselves performing and to determine their ideologies; i.e. how these teachers explained and justified the functions they performed in classrooms. In effect we compared greatness with failure and ignored the teachers in the middle whose practices might be deemed satisfactory or average.

The first thing we discovered was that most of the functions commonly engaged in by teachers do not discriminate between stars and failure/quitters. For example, both groups indicated they spent the same amount of time planning. It was only when we delved into precisely what they did when they planned that we noted any distinctions. Quitter/failures most common planning behaviors were marking papers and noting the pages in the texts they would cover with their classes the next day. Stars most typical planning behaviors involved gathering materials and planning activities which they would use to engage and involve their students. The ideology that undergirds this mid-range function was also different. Quitter/failures' planning focused on what they would do as teachers while stars' planning focused on what they would get the students to do. On the surface then, planning was a function that seemed common to both groups, but when examined in detail it proved to be a function that served different purposes and involved the teacher in performing entirely different behaviors.

THE RESEARCH BASE OF STAR TEACHER FUNCTIONS

As a result of the tests, observations, and interviews in these trials, we identified fourteen mid-range functions that discriminated between stars and quitter/failures. These are functions which stars perform which quitter/failures never do and vice versa. The next stage was to create questions which would enable us to identify these distinctive functions and their undergirding ideology before individuals began to actually teach.

In the nine years of the National Teacher Corps (1963-1972) we put approximately 1,500 interns through the University of Wisconsin Milwaukee Teacher Intern program. During this period we interviewed approximately 3,000 candidates and were able to perfect the interview through annual trials and follow-up of graduates' performance in urban classrooms. For all the interns who passed through the program we were able to assess the interview against their subsequent performance, their ability to relate to children and their retention rates. As a result of these annual replications the interview was refined into its present form. Since 1972, I have conducted seven trials around the country replicating the original design, i.e. having stars and quitter/failures identify their mid-range functions and ideologies. The last of these was in Florida in 2001. In all cases the original seven mid-range functions have stood up and been identified as discriminating; i.e. functions which stars perform that quitter/failures never do and vice versa. We have never identified a personality profile that describes star teachers: some stars are aggressive while others are shy; some are business-like and others warm, some are more focused on organization and others on creativity. But the mid-range functions and their undergirding ideology have remained the same over forty-five years.

Although there were 14 mid-range functions which discriminated between stars and quitter/failures we were never able to develop questions that would allow us to validly and reliably assess the candidates' predispositions to perform seven of these. The Star Teacher Urban Interview Questionnaire, therefore, utilizes only seven of the total number of mid-range functions that discriminate between stars and quitter/failures. All fourteen of the functions are explained in the subsequent sections of this volume.

STAR TEACHERS

Validity and Reliability

The instrument predicts who will stay in urban schools as classroom teachers for longer than three years. It predicts the success of the teachers as measured by the ratings of other constituencies in their school settings (administrators, teachers, staff, external experts, parents, students and themselves). It predicts the effectiveness of teachers in terms of their students' learning, on all grade levels, in all subject matters and in all areas of exceptional education. It predicts other things as well. The number of males and people of color brought into teaching has markedly increased; in some cases five times the typical rate. The instrument predicts the teachers' ability to relate to diverse children and youth in urban poverty schools. Passing the interview identifies teachers whose students subsequently have higher attendance rates and teachers who suspend and expel almost no students while teaching in schools where more than half of the students are suspended each year. Finally, the interview predicts teacher staying power.

As of this writing, approximately 170 urban school districts use the interview to screen and hire teachers new to their districts. Throughout the United States over 30,000 new teachers are hired each year using the interview. Each of these districts keeps their own records of their teacher evaluations so that the claims made here are all independent, objective assessments and are not simply the "biased" views of the writer. In a recent follow-up of 137 teachers who had completed my own intern program we found that ninety-four percent of them were still teaching in the Milwaukee Public Schools eight years later, that seventy-six percent were teachers of color and that fewer than five percent had ratings of less than satisfactory by their principals. These results are highly significant in a district where fifty percent of the beginners who deign to try urban teaching leave in three years or less and where fewer than five percent are teachers of color.

Five of the seven functions assessed on the interview can be readily observed in teachers' classroom practice. In a multiple regression analysis these five items explained the following variance in scores.

	Variance	Cumulated
Interview question #4	.21	
Interview question #1	.13	.24
Interview question #2	.12	.46
Interview question #7	.08	.54
Interview question #6	.05	.59

The mid-range functions assessed on the interview discriminate completely between stars and quitter/failures. Ninety percent of quitter/failures fail the interview and ninety-five percent of stars pass. This level of discrimination reflects how the instrument was developed. Functions that stars perform that quitter/failures never do (and vice versa) was the level of acceptance for each of the factors.

The predictive validity of the interview is assessed by following candidates into practice. The findings of our studies, as well as the reports of the 170 cities which use the interview indicate that, if conducted appropriately, the interview will have a ninety-five percent level of success. Only one in twenty of those who pass will be quitter/failure teachers. This compares with a fifty percent rate of success for graduates of traditional programs. Actually there is significantly less than a fifty percent retention rate of those from traditional programs since only ten percent of graduates of traditional university programs even apply to be teachers in the 120 urban districts serving 7,000,000 children in poverty…and since half of these ten percent quit or fail in five years or less the actual rate at which traditional programs of teacher education supply urban districts is approximately five percent of those they graduate and dub, "fully qualified".

All those who pass the interview have the predispositions to succeed as urban teachers serving diverse students in poverty. The differences in scores among candidates who pass predict two things about them: how quickly they will demonstrate specific competencies and how much mentoring they will require to reach the proficiency levels of effective teachers. Since candidates who fail the interview are not admitted, we study predictive validity among failure/quitters by assessing veteran teachers who identify themselves as quitter/failures. These are teachers leaving urban districts for private, small town or suburban schools, or who leave teaching entirely. Quitter/failure samples are not difficult to secure since they typically regard the schools and the children as failures rather than themselves. They are pleased to conduct exit interviews and willingly offer their views of what is wrong with the systems they are leaving. Essentially, they are correct in the sense that these school systems are failing but incorrect in blaming the victims. What the failure/quitter teachers do not allow themselves to understand is that other teachers are experiencing success with the very same students under the very same negative conditions of work that they regard as impossible. In the eleven follow-up studies of failure/quitter teachers which I have conducted we have interviewed over 234 teachers in six cities. Only twenty-six failure/quitters individuals have passed the interview. These were individuals who gave their reasons for leaving as "maternity" or "family moving out of state."

The reliability of the instrument has been assessed in two ways: will two interviewers of the same candidate score that candidate in the same way and will the same candidate being interviewed over and over make the same score? The likelihood that a candidate who is interviewed a second, third, fourth or more times will make the same score is r =.93.   A colleague and I have personally interviewed the same candidates up to six times in successive years and found no change in their scores. The likelihood that two interviewers will learn to score the interview in the same way has been studied in-depth in multiple settings with principals, teachers, human resource personnel and parents serving as interviewers. Among all constituencies, if two interviewers have six interviews together their scores become interchangeable; that is, the scores of one interviewer predict the scores of his/her partner. As part of their training, individuals learning to interview are encouraged to have six trial interviews with their partners before conducting real interviews of candidates.

During the development of the interview questions have been raised about the possibility of cultural bias of the mid-range functions. Several specific subgroups have been tested to determine whether the distribution of scores is the same as for European Americans: male and female Latinos; military retirees; veteran teachers who graduated from traditional programs of teacher certification; male and female African Americans; Southeast Asians from Laos and Cambodia; and foreign teachers from Russia, Israel, Mexico, Australia and New Zealand. In all cases the distribution of scores does not differ from those of European Americans. In the case of African Americans, there is a positive, non-significant difference in the number who passes. The interview has also been tested as a predictor of candidates by grade level, subject matter and teacher of children with special needs. There are no differences among these specializations in terms of the interview's power to predict interviewees' scores on any of the seven scales or subscales.

Age does predict differences in interview scores. Among candidates over thirty years of age one in three who present themselves as wanting to teach diverse children in urban poverty passes the interview. Of those under twenty-five years of age who make the same claim one in ten passes. Those between twenty-five and thirty years of age have a pass rate of one in eight. Clearly, the predispositions needed to teach diverse children in poverty are related to development and life experiences. This does not mean that all mature adults who seek to teach in poverty schools can learn to do so since only one in three of these applicants passes. Similarly, while only one in ten of those under twenty-five passes, ten percent represents 50,000 youngsters in the annual pool of graduates from traditional teacher education who do have the potential to teach diverse youngsters in urban poverty. What these findings mean is that, while no population of teacher candidates should be dismissed solely on the basis of age, the more mature the pool of candidates the greater the likelihood that more will pass the interview.

There has been a unique legal validation of the Star Urban Teacher Selection Interview. In an exhaustive evaluation of the instrument, a jury considered the evidence supporting the interview and the testimony of the writer and other educational experts (Rodriguez vs. The Chicago Board of Education, 1996). The jury's verdict was that 1) it was fair and equitable to use the interview to hire teachers for the Chicago Public Schools, and 2) because the Chicago Public Schools hired a teacher with a lower score than Mr. Rodriguez he was entitled to damages.

Using the same mid-range functions that discriminate between stars and quitter/failures, a short answer, self administered, fifty item pre-screener has been developed. Candidates take this test on-line. Those who pass are more likely to pass the complete interview. The correlation between scores on the pre-screener and the interview is r =.72. It is now common for several great

93

cities and the military dealing with large numbers of applicants to use the pre-screener to limit the number of applicants who will need to be personally interviewed.

Some of the Ph.D. dissertations utilizing the Star Teacher Selection Interview include:

1. Lesniak, R.J. "Predicting Classroom Behavior of Urban Teacher Candidates Through the Use of a Classroom Behavior Task". Syracuse University, 1969
2. Storey, R. "Selecting Candidates for the Army-Baylor Physical Therapy Program". University of Texas, 1994
3. Chesek, F. "Attributes that Predict the De-escalation of Violence". Loyola University (Chicago) 1994
4. Teske, L. "Supplementing Haberman's Mid-range Functions". UCLA,1999.
5. Fostiak, M. "The Reliability of the Star Urban Teacher Selection Interview in Determining the Classroom Success of Elementary Teachers". Loyola University (Chicago), 2000
6. McKinney, S. "An Inquiry Into the Internship Experience and Development of Effective Urban Teacher Characteristics of Interns in Urban Professional Development Schools". Old Dominion University, 2001
7. Pillow-Price, K. "Evaluation of the Haberman Urban Teacher Selection Interview in Rural School Settings". Arkansas State University, 2003

The research supporting the interview has now transcended the level of predicting the effectiveness and staying power of individual teacher candidates and has become a basis for moving schools off urban district's lists of failing schools or Schools In Need of Improvement. In the Buffalo Creek School in Spring Branch, a Houston elementary school serving primarily Mexican-American children in poverty and the Highgate Heights elementary school in Buffalo, New York serving primarily African American children in poverty, the interview has been used as a school improvement strategy. These were failing schools which were given the opportunity to reconstitute themselves. The entire faculty of these schools, including veteran as well as new teachers, was selected on the basis of passing the interview. In both cases the achievement scores of the students went from schools that were officially designated as failing to among the highest achieving schools in their respective districts in one year.

Chapter XI
The Ideology of Stars

In order to fully comprehend what star teachers do it is necessary to understand the ideology which undergirds their behaviors. The very same behaviors performed by teachers who do not have positive relationships with their students will engender entirely different responses when performed by teachers who do have positive relationships. It is typical for immature students learning to teach to ask, "Why don't they just tell me what to do and I'll do it!" To overcome the naivety of this question and help neophytes understand the full nature of what they think they are observing, I have taken them to visit a local middle school where I know there are both star and quitter/leaver teachers. During the first period we observe a teacher who might say to a student, "Jerome, please sit down and finish your work." The student responds with profanity, by leaving the room or by continuing to wander around but never by doing any work. The bell rings and we follow the same class of children to the second hour. Here a different teacher may say to the same child, "Jerome, please sit down and finish your work." In this case the student complies and spends the period producing a paper that shows both effort and progress.

Are we to interpret "Please sit down and finish your work." as a "best practice"? Shall those learning to teach memorize this brilliant sentence to use on the future Jeromes they will most certainly meet? Can there be "best practices" apart from the specific teacher who engages in the particular behavior with a particular student? Can there be "best practices" which are independent of the nature of the relationship the teacher has established with the student?" There are no practices which exist independently of the teacher-student relationship. The very same behaviors and comments which work for some teachers will actually cause problems for others. Again, the neophyte interprets this difference in student reaction to mean that it is all a question of the teacher's personality, or idiosyncrasy, or worst of all, that effective teachers are born with a magical something. What stars have is an ideology that undergirds everything they say and do. This ideology communicates to students and is the basis of a bonding relationship that makes everything work. For this reason most who visit classrooms to observe do not "see" because the basis of the teacher's ability to relate to the students is an ideology ...and this ideology is only knowable after in-depth observations over time and personal conferences with the teacher. Great insight into the effectiveness of star teachers' can be derived from understanding what they believe about the following three issues: What is the role of the school serving diverse children in poverty? What is the teacher's expectation regarding having problem students? And how do stars explain what causes students to be successful?

A. The Role of the School Serving Diverse Children in Poverty

For children in poverty being successful in school is a matter of life and death. For those without a high school diploma the likelihood of ever having a decent job—one with adequate health insurance and some form of retirement account---is extremely remote. Being a drop-out or a push-out dooms people to dead-end jobs, living in unsafe neighborhoods, and never being able to fully provide adequate health care for themselves and their families. It also means that those who are miseducated never develop the individual potentialities that would give their lives greater meaning and society the benefit of their participation and productivity.

Effective teachers of diverse children and youth in poverty act as if their work were comparable to others engaged in occupations involving the life and death of their clients. Stars believe that everyday they involve their students in learning important subject matter; they are, in effect, saving them from lives of desperation and unfulfilled promise. This means that they not only find their work rewarding but also stressful. Stressful because star teachers recognize they do not control all the out-of-school and life experiences that impinge on student achievement, but they still accept accountability for their students' learning. They know the very high stakes involved for the children and for society. Given this understanding of how stars view the purpose of schools serving diverse children in poverty clarifies why star teachers work with urgency and under stress; they do not perceive of teaching as simply a pleasant occupation. Once they take on the responsibility for the life and death of their students, and they do, the job becomes a calling to which they make a total commitment. Star teachers of diverse children in poverty can more accurately be described as life savers than as pedagogues. Unfortunately for children and youth, many teachers go through entire programs of preparation and actually take jobs before they fully appreciate the pressure and stress that accompanies accepting accountability. Teachers who perceive of themselves as teaching some basic skills for four or five hours and then "having a life" outside, perform an entirely different job than those who believes they are engaged in the business of saving lives.

The individual who perceives the goal of schools serving children and youth in poverty as helping them learn basic skills is certainly correct. But if this goal becomes the only goal it is a limited view of the teacher's work and inevitably leads to a narrowing of the curriculum and a lowering of expectations. Star teachers believe that their primary goal is turning kids on—i.e. engaging them in becoming lifelong learners. They value transmitting important content and subject matter, but they regard the need for children to learn more as the means to even higher goals, i.e. the development of individual talents, greater self esteem, commitment to service and citizenship, and the well-being that comes from becoming a lifelong learner of various realms of knowledge. Stars believe the comprehensive goals of schooling expected of advantaged learners in well-endowed communities and schools should be expected of diverse children in poverty.

The subject of various dissertations and numerous articles has been "What do Americans want their children to get out of thirteen years of schooling?" The typical lists that are generated from such questions include the following goals:

- basic skills and information,
- principles and concepts of important subject matter disciplines,
- skills in problem solving, critical thinking and making independent judgments,

- the knowledge base and commitment required to participate as an active citizen,
- the knowledge base and skills for practicing personal health,
- the knowledge base and commitment to protect the environment,
- aesthetic development in the practice and appreciation of fine arts,
- character—the development and practice of ethical, moral behavior,
- a positive self concept,
- the development of individual talents and abilities,
- basic skills, knowledge and attitudes for succeeding in the world of work.

These eleven goals and others are cited by over seventy-five percent of the public for their own children. However, when parents and the community at large are asked about the goals of the schools for other people's children; that is, for the fourteen million diverse children and youth in poverty, the whole list is telescoped and cut down to "get a job and stay out of jail." It is not an accident of history or chance that vocational high schools are in city school systems and not in suburban or small town districts. In many urban areas "career education" is introduced as early as kindergarten. American opinion is moving more and more in the direction of European and Asian systems which use testing to decide by age eleven which children will go into vocational education and which to the university for advanced studies and professional training. Such early screening and tracking is supported on the grounds that it is what society needs and the best way to keep poor youngsters out of the criminal justice system.

While Americans believe this limited view of schooling is appropriate for those in poverty they believe in a much more open approach for middle class and affluent children. This view argues that many children are late bloomers. Many people don't decide to go to college until age thirty or beyond and doors should be held open for them. They argue that many who attend the university as late adolescents and young adults are too immature to derive the full benefits of the experience and as a result drop out or do poorly. These individuals should be given another chance after they mature. The fundamental American value is that individuals of all ages should have the opportunity to change jobs, careers and professions at any age and there should be some college or university available to help them do so. As a result, there are over 2,200 colleges, an equal number of junior, community and two year colleges and an increasing number of on-line universities offering preparation for every conceivable job and profession. In this remarkable array, where every form of education is offered to people of all ages, the narrowing and limiting of the public school's goals for diverse children in poverty is particularly unfair and demeaning. As Jeannie Oakes and other researchers have demonstrated, school tracking is clearly the process for keeping low-income people in low level jobs. It also keeps them in schools where less is taught and less is learned because the goals of these schools have been narrowed and lowered.

Without using the jargon of academe, star teacher are avid proponents of a full, rich arts and science curriculum for all students. They know that children come to school extremely curious about the world around them. They are naturally scientists. Paul Torrence in his studies of creativity found that five year olds were in the ninetieth percentile on tests of creativity. By age fifteen the same population of children was assessed as being in the bottom five percent on tests of creativity. What happened to these children? Where were these children between ages five and fifteen? What were these children taught during this period that destroyed their creativity?

Stars know and act on the belief that the primary concern of young children is searching for explanations of how the world works. Children begin as open-minded artists and scientists eager and ready to participate in the world of learning. Stars act as if they truly believe that children in poverty can and should learn as much as possible in the widest array of subject matters. The greatest arts and science teachers are not the faculty in the most prestigious universities but star teachers in elementary and secondary schools serving diverse children and youth in poverty.

Star teachers believe that offering the broad goals of schooling typically reserved for affluent children of privilege to children in poverty is a matter of equity and justice. Unfortunately, the dumbed down curriculum of "get a job and stay out of jail" held by the public is also supported by many teachers working with diverse children in poverty. This narrowing of the curriculum inevitably leads to the lowering of standards and expectations. If teachers of students in poverty believed they were preparing their students for careers such as a brain surgeon, governor, business leader or inventor they would require and expect them to learn important knowledge to advanced levels. But the jobs that have become the goals of the narrowed, dumbed-down curriculum of schools serving children in poverty are typically focused on service industries always in need of employees for dead-end jobs without career ladders. These are also the jobs that can be performed with little training and on less than a full-time basis. One of the greatest errors poor teachers make is to perceive of their students as future adults performing in specific low level occupations. These perceptions form the basis for their lowered expectations which in turn guide all their interactions with students. In effect, the lowered expectations become a self-fulfilling prophecy. By seeing their students as future menials, poor teachers systematically deliver a watered-down curriculum which ensures that little of much value will be learned in school. As a result, their students are systematically led to believe that learning is never engaging, important, or the means for transforming their lives.

Star teachers never fall into the trap of believing they can predict the future lives and occupations of their students. They assume their students have unknown and unlimited potentialities. Star teachers believe their students are not only as smart as they are but are more likely to learn more in the future than their teachers now know. This leads them to respond to students in ways which are not only respectful but highly motivational...and such behaviors also become a self-fulfilling prophecy. Successful and outstanding individuals who grew up in poverty inevitably point to particular teachers who transformed their lives with the high expectations that led to their learning of advanced forms of knowledge. The difference between stars and poor teachers, therefore, is not just in the different expectations they hold for their students but in the actual content they teach because they hold different visions of students' potentialities. Star teachers push students to ever more advanced levels of important forms of knowledge. Poor teachers' limited vision of their students' in low-level, dead end jobs (or in the criminal justice system) leads them to narrow and dumb-down the curriculum until it is essentially the endless repetition of low level skills which lead students to view learning as having little value or relevance. My observations in urban schools serving diverse children in urban poverty for over half a century are a constant reminder of the endless "basic skills" taught to students over and over at every grade level...which never seem to be mastered. In urban schools serving diverse students in poverty, the lessons being taught involve the same material being taught to high school students as to primary children, e.g. how to write and punctuate a simple sentence, basic arithmetic skills, remembering things in order, writing a clear explanation of something, and the almost literal recall of things just read. It is heartbreaking to see thirteen years of school devoted to the endless pounding of the same low level skills into students who have become inured, detached and resistant to the process.

Star teachers engage their students in the learning of important subject matter. They hold no preconceived, limiting notions of what their students can learn or might become in life. They don't think of school as merely preparation for living but as living now. As a consequence, their teaching becomes relevant, alive and meaningful. Poor teachers see skills as prerequisite to learning important concepts later and as a result never get beyond the teaching of skills; and therefore, never get to teaching any subject matter at advanced levels. Star teachers understand that learning important concepts motivates students to learn the skills needed to go further and deeper. They teach skills along with advanced concepts and ideas. In contrast to the classrooms of poor teachers, locked in and frozen on drill and kill, I am constantly impressed by the high level and advanced concepts star teachers are able to teach to children of all ages and even those labeled with handicapping conditions. Poor teachers think they know the potentialities of their students. Stars regard such beliefs as presumptuous and an impediment to teaching.

B. The Expectation of Problems

All professions involve serving clients with particular problems. Those who become practitioners understand that it is in the nature of any profession to deal with people who have problems. Those who become dentists do not expect to practice dentistry by only giving examinations to those with perfect teeth and advice to only those who will follow it. A dentist regards it as a natural condition of his/her work to be dealing with people who have bad teeth and bad gums and who are not always overjoyed about their treatment. Many clients may even have contagious diseases which make the dentist's work dangerous. By definition, it is not possible to practice dentistry and avoid people with dental problems. This analogue pertains to all professionals. Lawyers deal with clients who present them with legal problems, many of which involve the stress of avoiding prison sentences. It is not people who are free of legal problems who seek the services of lawyers but those with serious problems. Accountants, social workers and health professionals all deal with people who face issues which they need help dealing with. Professionals expect and prepare for serving people who have problems because they would not have a professional practice if their clients did not bring them their problems. Indeed, it is to the advantage of professionals to have clients with problems. The greater the number and complexity of the problems the more money they make…and the greater the satisfaction they derive from helping their clients deal with these problems.

Why is pointing out such obvious things about professional practice necessary? Why, in a book about teaching is there a need to point out that people enter professions because they want to deal with problems? Why is there a need to remind people that the practice of any profession continuously involves the practitioner in dealing with conditions and issues that need fixing? The answer is that the criterion too many young people use to decide that teaching is appropriate for them is that they "love children" not that they want to deal with children's needs and problems all day, everyday. Unfortunately, love is not enough. It is not a method of teaching and not a goal of the schools. This distorted basis for entering professional service continues on into the practice of veteran teachers. It is demonstrated by the fact that teachers make sure that students defined as being problems or having problems are equally distributed. They protest or feel unfairly treated if they have more inclusion students than the teacher next door. They resent having more students who are below grade level than other teachers. Indeed, many teachers will protest if they have more male students than other teachers. The term teachers use for being assigned children with problems is being "dumped on". The objective is to avoid problems, or to have as few problems as possible. In effect, teachers prefer to teach children who don't really need them. Their expectation is that if the system were working the way it should be they would only have children who complete assignments without having the instructions repeated over and over, and that the children would all complete their assignments without continuous monitoring. They hold on to this fantasy even in the face of years of experience and continue to practice the Pedagogy of Poverty described earlier. Many teachers enter the profession not understanding that professionals are needed precisely for the purpose of dealing with problems and they maintain this irrational belief throughout their careers by seeking to have other teachers, specialists or aides deal with their problems.

Star teachers do not think this way. Their ideology is the reverse. They understand that, like other professionals, they are there to perform services which help children and youth deal with all kinds of problems that interfere with their learning. This component of the star teacher's ideology is critical to their success and in understanding the differences between them and failure/quitters. Failure/quitters define any child who interferes with their giving of a lesson, or who is unable or unwilling to follow the directions for completing the assignment as a problem...a problem that the teacher should not be having. The best "solution" that quitter/failures see for these problems is either removing the student or having someone else (with more time or special training) deal with student problems. They do not accept the role of problem solver because in their view of the teacher's role, students with problems should not be there. This belief that the ideal teaching situation is a problem-free classroom leads to a bizarre situation for substantial numbers of teachers working with diverse children in poverty. They are under constant stress because they will inevitably be assigned many students with severe problems and troubling previous school experiences. And in spite of the realities they face daily, they will cling to the view that their role as teachers is to have as few problems as possible. This explains why so many teachers persist in believing that the children in their classrooms, in many cases a majority of them, should not be there. As a consequence of this widespread denial of what constitutes professional service, diverse students in urban poverty schools are either suspended or mislabeled as abnormal in disproportionate numbers. In my city, high schools have an annual suspension rate of sixty-five percent, middle schools an annual rate of fifty percent and elementary schools an annual rate of twenty percent. In a typical year 180 children are suspended from kindergarten! In this district twenty percent of the students are labeled as cognitively disabled, emotionally disturbed, learning disabled or with some other handicapping condition.

In the 120 urban school districts across the country, teachers are unable to accept that the nature of "professional" work is to deal with problems. The non-professional expectations of those trained in traditional university based programs (i.e. the "fully qualified") who do not want to deal with student problems or problem students, is a fundamental cause for a majority of diverse children in poverty achieving below grade level, for a majority of male youth being suspended at some time in their school careers, for only half of African American and Latino students graduating from high school, and for one-fifth or more of the children being labeled abnormal.

C. Effort versus Ability

The way star teachers explain success is critical to understanding their ideology and their teaching behaviors. If quitter/failure teachers are asked to explain what accounts for some children being successful in school while others are not, they refer to ability. It is obvious to them that some children are smart, some average and others slow. Quitter/failure teachers completely buy into the notion that there is a general intelligence factor that everyone is born with and that native ability is the best explanation for success in school and in life. Star teachers eschew this explanation. They know that in school, as in all walks of life, the best explanation of success is effort.

This is a critical distinction. It leads to star teachers, in effect, performing a different job than poor teachers. Those who rely on ability as the explanation of success believe they will have little influence in effecting how much their students learn. They see their job as essentially presenting subject matter and then sorting, tracking and grading students. Those who believe that effort explains success see their job as trying to generate more student work. When poor teachers are asked what they actually do when they plan for teaching, they talk about covering material that they believe reflects the abilities of their students. When stars are asked what they do when they plan, they reply that they spend most of their time looking for engaging activities and materials that will motivate their students to participate fully and try harder.

Star teachers are obsessed with generating effort. It is part of everything they do. They know that success in their own college careers and in the world of work was a reflection of the effort they expended not their ability. They also believe that the same is true for all people in all walks of life. Success is more frequently and more closely associated with effort than with inherent ability. This component of the star ideology is especially powerful among star secondary teachers. By high school age, many students explain success in school, and in life, in terms of ability, luck, family connections and knowing the right people. High school students are prone to overlook or deny the effort and persistence that is expended by those they define and admire as successful. By adolescence these misconceptions are also sex-linked. When males do well they tend to explain success in terms of their ability. If they do poorly they explain failure in terms of poor effort, i.e. not caring enough to try. In their value scheme the best result is to do well with no effort or study whatever. For females it tends to be the reverse. When they do well they say it is because they studied and when they do poorly they attribute it to a lack of ability. In the female value scheme, therefore, effort explains success and they strengthen their commitment to study as they go further. These differences explain why females earn higher grades in college even though they may score lower on SAT's and other supposed predictors of success in higher education.

Star teachers demonstrate their commitment to eliciting, fostering and rewarding effort in their daily teaching, in the way they grade and in the way they discuss their students' work with parents and with the students themselves. The star ideology considers no alternative to this commitment. Consider the impact on students' lives if they reach adulthood believing in ability without effort. Consider the lifelong effect on students if they believe that success in life is a function of luck or who you know. For many youth this distorted view of how success is achieved is already dominant in middle school. In the studies teachers and I have conducted with middle school students on how they explain success, students doing poorly or on the verge of dropping out will respond in ways that make it clear they explain success in terms of factors other than effort. Their lack of understanding the need for sustained effort is also illustrated by their aspirations. When middle school students with third grade level basic skills are asked about their life goals they frequently respond with jobs such as astronaut or brain surgeon.

Star teachers eschew psychometry. They place no credence whatever on any form of "scientific" assessment of youngsters' abilities or potentialities. They do not believe that educational psychologists, or anyone else, can predict how much or what children can learn. While they recognize that some children suffer from disabling conditions, they believe that living and working with children on a daily basis provides them with more valid knowledge about those children than any formal psychological assessments. Stars are not impressed by scores on intelligence, personality and aptitude tests in their students' records. They are likely to ignore such scores and enjoy demonstrating that they are inaccurate predictors.

The ideology of star teachers is very much centered in their commitment to the concept of individual differences and to the immeasurable potential of all people if given sufficient encouragement and opportunity. The whole notion of predicting in advance how much people can learn is antithetic to their very being. They reject the objective, scientific measurement approach in favor of an existential commitment that says, "No one can possibly know in what directions and how far developing individuals might grow."

D. Direct Instruction

There is substantial evidence that the achievement of children in poverty improves markedly when they are taught with direct instruction. The problem is, what is meant by "direct instruction"? Direct instruction is not "There's the assignment, get at it." Giving a class an assignment and then monitoring compliance is not a form of instruction at all but the Pedagogy of Poverty described in Chapter VIII. Unfortunately, many teachers confuse teaching with giving directions and then disciplining those who do not comply. Simply making assignments, giving directions and monitoring compliance is neither direct instruction nor teaching.

Many researchers and teachers defend directive, highly structured teacher behavior by pointing to the fact that children in poverty frequently live lives with few controls and little structure. They argue that it is common for many children who grow up in poverty to be left to their own devices. At the same time it is not unusual for children who may be neglected to live with adults who relate to them in only authoritarian ways where "might makes right." Given these living conditions children arrive in kindergarten needing structure in their lives and new ways to relate to adults. If children are conditioned to only listen to people who make them do things it takes time and systematic weaning to move them from only giving respect and attention to those who can overpower them. This view of the teacher as a highly structured taskmaster is supported by studies of youngsters in poverty who, when asked to describe their best teacher, say "Ms. X. She made us learn."

It is certainly true that many youngsters in poverty come to school and are faced with rules and routines for the first time in their lives. It is also true that beginning in kindergarten the teachers' job is to put some consistent structure into their lives that children can depend upon. This is where learning in school starts—with where the learners are—but it is not where it should end. The goal of thirteen years of schooling is to have children develop into people who will be committed to lifelong learning, even when there are no longer any teachers around to supervise and control them. The goal is to have internally motivated people who will be able to think independently and critically. Being told what to do all day only leads to the game of "try and make me" which characterizes student behavior in failed schools in poverty areas. In the game of "try and make me" the children will always win and the teachers will always be under stress trying to force compliance among children with no interest in what they are doing. But worst of all, the internal motivators will never be developed. If the instructional strategies used are limited to controlling and overpowering children, they learn to not read unless someone supervises, to never write anything unless it is assigned, and to take no interest in science or math unless it is a required school activity. The danger of getting short term achievement results from telling, directing and mandating student behavior is that the long term goals of making students independent, critical thinking, lifelong learners is lost.

Direct instruction is a legitimate method of teaching. It is not the same as giving directions all day. Stars use it as one method, not the only form of instruction. The seven parts of the direct instruction methodology go far beyond direction-giving and monitoring compliance. The components of this method are as follows:

1. Anticipatory Set. This occurs when students are arriving or shifting gears. The teacher a) focuses the students' attention; b) provides a quick practice on previous, related learning, and c) develops a readiness, i.e. tunes the class in for what will follow. This part of the lesson is very

brief.

2. Objective and Its Purpose. In this step the teacher informs the students what they will be able to do by the end of the activity. The teacher explains what they will accomplish and why it will be useful and relevant in their present and future lives. This part of the lesson is very brief.

3. Instructional Input. In this step the teacher selects the means for "getting it into the students' heads". Will it be the teacher talking, a book, film, or demonstration? This step could also involve student discovery. This part of the lesson is longer than steps 1, 2, or 3 but still less than 10 minutes.

4. Modeling. In this step students must see examples. This part of the lesson has some visual input. The teacher models something concrete. If it is a concept being taught the teacher may say, "I'll tell you what I'm thinking as I work this." This step takes between five and ten minutes.

5. Checking for Understanding. The teacher needs to check if the students get it. This can be done in three ways: a) posing questions; b) requesting signaled responses from students; or c) getting written responses. This step takes about five minutes.

6. Guided Practice. Students' initial attempts must be carefully guided so that they are accurate and successful. The teacher circulates among students and provides help. This step is the longest part of any lesson and can last up to fifteen minutes.

7. Independent Practice. Once the students can perform the task with the teacher they must practice independently with little or no teacher direction. This can be checked in class but also performed as homework. This step takes less than five minutes of class time.

These seven steps are rarely performed by those who claim to be using "direct instruction." When all the steps are performed with skill there is no question that direct instruction can be one of several effective method of teaching diverse children in urban poverty. Star teachers use this method as they deem appropriate for the particular content they are teaching. It is also important to note that star teachers use all the methods and are not locked into any one. They also use independent study, computer assisted instruction, cooperative learning, peer tutoring and the project method. It is accurate to state that I know of no star teachers who limit themselves to only

Chapter XII
The Mid-Range Functions of Stars Which Cannot Be Assessed in Interviews
A. Emotional/physical Stamina

Life in the classroom does not occur in semesters, months, weeks or even hours. It consists of intense episodes of a few minutes, or sometimes even a few seconds. A teacher's day has literally hundreds of rapid-fire interactions, many of them occurring at the same time. To say that it is draining is to refer to Niagara Falls as damp.

Stamina is a quality frequently taken for granted unless it is lacking. Consider first the quality of emotional stamina. Teachers frequently deal with children who have been neglected and abused. As the children grow star teachers also deal with issues of drugs, gangs, pregnancy and the criminal justice system. It is quite typical for star teachers to develop close relationships with children that include out-of-school contacts. Star teachers have appeared in court on behalf of their students. I recently worked with a star teacher who sat up all night with a seventh grader who was having a baby. Not all these contacts necessarily end happily or positively. Sometimes these teachers attend the funerals of their students or end up visiting them in hospitals or in prison. It requires a great deal of emotional stamina to teach all day and to invest additional time and energy in children outside of school. It requires even more emotional stamina when a student in whom the teacher has invested a great deal of time regresses back into negative practices. It is at such times that the meaning of emotional stamina is demonstrated. When disappointed by a particular student in whom they have invested caring, time and energy stars do not give up or change their pattern of trying to help their students respond to life problems. I have known them to attend the funeral of a child in the evening and be back at work the next morning. They are able to go on, reach out and support children regardless of the disappointments. They do not allow themselves to be defeated by the youngster they may be giving extra time to who drops out and disappears, or the girl who becomes pregnant a second time, or the boy who is seriously wounded in a gang fight. They keep trying to help and draw strength from the successes. They relate to their children on a close, personal basis. Where others would be defeated, e.g. "You can't help these kids; they never appreciate what you do and just lapse back," star teachers keep involving themselves in the lives of their students because they have both the commitment and the emotional stamina. Physical stamina is more familiar and easier to describe. This stamina undergirds the enthusiasm that is readily observable in the teacher's daily behavior. Stars—as opposed to burnouts—are vitally "into" whatever they teach. Their enthusiasm for the subject, the activity, and the children's responses are all intertwined. Stars never go through the motions of covering material to uninvolved students. They have endless energy and enthusiasm. They give their students the impression that things they have done countless times before are being done for the first time and that the student responses they have heard for years are being heard for the first time.

In former time, those who sought to explain this attribute used terms such as "surging" or "dynamic personality". This is not a dimension of personality at all. Many star teachers do not demonstrate the same enthusiasm in other spheres of their lives that they show in their teaching. A basic principle of stars' teaching is, "You can't teach what you don't care about to people you don't care about." In listening to their explanations of what they think makes them successful, stars frequently refer to the "aha" reaction. They talk about the light in a child's eyes, a smile, even a child's gesture of triumph when a concept is grasped or a skill is mastered and demonstrated. Stars elicit and share this enthusiasm as some of their most cherished moments in teaching. They merge their enthusiasm for their children with their enthusiasm for their subject matter. As with other star functions, emotional stamina reflects their ideology. Stars believe that learning is synonymous with living and living is synonymous with growth. Therefore, when learning is at hand, growth is at hand. They believe learning is a natural act which students will pursue to achieve a sense of well being. I refer to this enthusiasm and energy as stamina because it reflects the behavior stars know they must demonstrate everyday, all day, if they are to serve as learning models for the children. Energy levels of children far exceed those of their adult teachers. This is natural and a fact of life. If teachers start responding to their needs rather than their students (i.e. in need of a break, a bit jaded or tired, coasting through an afternoon, etc.), what does this model for children and youth who are vibrant and alive every second? Stars' energy and enthusiasm is clearly a form of craft knowledge; they know they must demonstrate it to keep the students with them.

While stamina clearly discriminates between stars and quitter/failures, I have never been able to develop the questions and responses which would validly predict this behavior. I do not believe there are reasonable questions that can be asked in an interview that will accurately assess an individual's physical and emotional energy in future settings with specific groups of students. Until one is actually observed in the act of teaching in a specific setting for a sustained period it is not possible to evaluate this attribute. The inability to assess this function in an interview, however, does not make the attribute less critical to the success of teachers serving diverse children in poverty.

In a very real sense stamina is not a personal attribute as much as it is craft knowledge and part of the effective teacher's repertoire. Stars know that they must demonstrate enthusiasm, energy and commitment in order to engender these responses in the students. Regardless of how they feel on a particular day, as professionals, they must act as if everything they are teaching is of critical importance. Stars' stamina enables them to never succumb to being worn down by the children, by the bureaucracy, or by the repetition inherent in teaching. Functioning as if everything is new and exciting all the time is an exceptionally high standard of performance to demonstrate consistently... one that requires boundless energy.

B. Organizational ability

Star teachers have extraordinary organizational skills. They need this high level of managerial skills because they use a variety of instructional methods. For example, the project method and other forms of hands-on instruction that actively involve students require advanced organizational skills. There are frequently several different activities occurring simultaneously in the classrooms of star teachers. Very often children are working in teams or groups, each of which is engaged in different activities. It is also common for individual children to pursue independent activities on their own. What ordinary teachers might regard as too much activity or even chaos, star teachers can manage as a normal level of activity. The more different things that are happening simultaneously, the greater the demands on the teacher's organizational skills. One of the reasons stars can do this is that they can multitask, i.e. they can do several things at once and still perform them at a high level. One of the most common reasons teachers quit or fail is that they are unable to multitask. The inability to multitask is a more common inadequacy among men than women who fail as teachers.

Another critically important component of stars' organizational ability is the way they gather and use instructional materials, equipment and supplies. Stars do not teach primarily with chalk and blackboards to seated children all engaged in the same activity. Stars align how they use materials, equipment, space, time and the grouping of the children with the particular learning objectives they are trying to achieve. They are consciously aware that how they organize the classroom will control what is learned. Quitter/failures behave as if classroom organization has nothing to do with learning. At the end of the day, star teachers are able to reconstruct and summarize which children have spent how much time doing what, with whom, for what purpose, with which materials and with what results. The reason they complicate things with different students doing different things in the same space and time period is that they are trying to account for individual differences. This form of teaching requires a high level of teacher "with-it-ness", i.e. the teacher's ability to sense what is going on everywhere in the classroom, with all of the children, at all times. In contrast, quitter/failures do none of this; they "cover" the same required grade level material with the entire class, ignoring both the students who already know the material, as well as the students who can't even read it. Poor teachers justify the practice of ignoring individuals who are advanced learners as "teaching to the middle" and ignoring those below grade level as "maintaining standards". These are weak rationalizations for not having the organizational ability to meet individual needs in the same classroom by having different students doing different things.

Stars high level of organizational ability is also demonstrated outside of the classroom and even on field trips. They are able to manage large numbers of children in camping experiences, in museums, amusement parks, or traveling great distances by bus or airplane. I have observed effective teachers taking children on trips throughout the country and even abroad, through baggage checks, detection, waiting rooms, actual flying, baggage pickup, ground transportation and hotel check -in with less difficulty than poorly organized teachers have taking their classes to the toilet or to the lunchroom in their own building.

The skills of organization and management are interrelated with other skills of teaching. These skills include knowing which children can be depended on as helpers and establishing a high level of trust with them so that they not only take care of themselves but each other. Given the opportunity, some children can actually become co-teachers who help the class engage in simultaneous activities that must be synchronized. Star teachers are adept time managers. They can derive value (i.e. a learning benefit for the children) out of as little as ten, five or even three minutes of extra time. Stars interact with children as if the purpose of any activity is to get the children to do the work—the speaking, questioning, finding out, writing, measuring or constructing—while the teacher's job is to serve as a coach and resource to the children. Quitter/failure teachers behave as if teaching is an opportunity for them to rehearse what they already know in the presence of children... and punish anyone who doesn't listen.

As with the other mid-range functions, teachers' organizational behavior reflects their ideology. Stars believe very strongly that children in poverty need instruction which empowers them to value and control their learning and is not simply based on authoritarianism. The conditions under which many youngsters live and grow ensures that they begin school believing that "might makes right". They see power in some form, i.e. physical strength, or the power to enforce, or the power to deny vital necessities, as the primary basis upon which children and adults relate to each other. As a result, children in poverty begin school highly responsive to the receipt of rewards and punishments from bigger, stronger more powerful adults. This readiness fits nicely with teachers who seek to maintain control by doling out rewards and punishments. It is not an accident that behavior modification works best for preschoolers and children in primary grades. Children are small and young. Most still seek the approval of their teachers. They can be readily managed with external rewards for following directions. There is substantial research evidence that primary teachers are the most directive and the most effective at classroom management. While they smile a great deal, reward young children with snacks and help them with their zippers and clothing, over two-thirds of everything they say is a direction or order that must be complied with. In-depth classroom observations over sustained periods of time document the fact that early childhood teachers give three times the number of directions per hour than upper elementary, middle, or high school teachers. This style of teaching—constant teacher directions with food and teacher approval awarded for compliance—is now the standard pattern of instruction found in kindergarten and primary grades. It fits well with children in poverty since it meshes with their out of school experiences. If one follows directions and does as one is told there are pleasant rewards; if not, there is teacher disapproval and punishments. In my city the average teacher's annual out-of-pocket expenditures exceed $600 per year and the most commonly purchased items are food and other rewards. Upper elementary, middle school and high school teachers all pay a price for this directiveness in terms of more mature students' apathy and resistance.

Unfortunately, as the children get older, they become larger and stronger. They also become less inclined to please their teachers and more concerned with peer approval. The fact that they are also expected to sit for longer periods and remain inactive compounds the problem. Added to this is the fact that by the beginning of fourth grade the curriculum has taken on many more abstractions and intangible concepts than the concrete lessons of the primary grades. The expectation that standard English will be spoken and written is more typical in the upper grades. For example, young children can get by in primary grades with using nouns and without knowing the precise use of prepositions. A kindergartner who doesn't know the difference between "in" and "into" is not affected in any way. By fourth grade, however, the school curriculum deals with abstract concepts, not only nouns and the naming of things. A more abstract curriculum requires precision in how prepositions such as from, by, to, of, into and countless others are used. It is no longer possible to deal with concepts in arithmetic or explain a science demonstration without precision and clarity in the use of prepositions. This accounts for the well documented achievement split between advantaged and disadvantaged children when they get beyond third grade. The achievement scores of middle-class children continue to rise while the achievement of children in poverty flattens out. After half a century of this divergence in achievement between economic classes as they move from primary to upper elementary grades it should be clear that simply being rewarded for following teachers' directions will not lead to learning an increasingly abstract curriculum requiring the use of more precise language.

Observing and listening to stars has led me to understand that preschool and primary grade instruction only seems to work because 1) the content is extremely concrete and 2) teaching by directive matches the backgrounds of the children in poverty. Unfortunately for poor teachers, as the children become larger they are more willing and able to resist. As they become young adolescents they care less about pleasing teachers and more about pleasing peers. The influence of rewards and punishments from teachers they don't care about fades in comparison to the power of the rewards and punishments exerted on them by peers. Faced with increasingly abstract subject matter that they find less relevant and less concrete, it becomes easier to resist learning and gain peer approval than to keep trying to gain the approval of teachers they don't care about, or who may not care about them. In middle school the achievement gap continues to widen as students work with directive teachers. Teachers can't control students or interest them in learning, except on the days they have free McDonald's® tickets to hand out. Students are turned off to learning because they have been systematically taught that learning is something they make you do or reward you for. The concept of internal motivation to learn is essentially non-existent in urban middle schools.

The organizational skills required to conduct directive lessons are minimal, but the approach becomes less and less effective as the children get older and more resistant to receiving full days of directions. The difficulty in using only directive methods is that compliance becomes harder to achieve as the children get older. A teacher may be skilled in demonstrating the seven steps of direct instruction described in the preceding section, but completely unable to keep the students on task.

In contrast, star teachers are engaged in more complex forms of instruction that require the children to accept a new form of relationship with teachers and others in positions of authority. In starting with a new class even stars must offer primarily direct instruction at the outset and gradually build the children up to longer and longer periods of self-determined activity. The first months in which stars work with children who have previously had only direct instruction are extremely difficult and trying for both teachers and children. The teacher is very uncomfortable with being forced into an authoritarian role by the children. The children are very leery of teachers trying to interest them rather then just making assignments and monitoring compliance. In working with children who have only known direct instruction, even stars are sometimes not able to get them to take responsibility for their own learning until the winter break.

Stars are adept at direct instruction because they must know how to begin where the children are and because some forms of content are offered best using this method. But they are also skilled at the project method, cooperative learning, thematic teaching, computer assisted instruction, peer tutoring, independent study, inquiry training, demonstrations, creative activities and scientific experimentation. To stars, using only direct instruction would be like having a tool box with only a hammer in it. While they begin with where the children are, they have the organizational skills to move the children to forms of learning that require intrinsic rather than extrinsic motivation. But without the undergirding organizational skills, teachers are unable to use the full range of methods needed to account for students' individual differences. I have never known a star teacher without a high level of organizational ability or a quitter/failure who excelled in this function.

C. The Nature of Planning

Stars and quitter/failures cannot be distinguished on the basis of how much time they report using for planning; the difference is in terms of what they do when they plan. Stars don't plan by focusing on what they will be doing but on what the children will be doing—alone, in groups or as a whole. When asked, "What do you actually do when you plan?" the differences between stars and quitter/failures become clear and significant. Quitter/failures mark papers, read over material they will be teaching and write down the books and pages they will be covering in their plan books. They also prepare handouts they will be assigning for classwork or homework. Stars' planning is a process of gathering materials and equipment and thinking of how they will get specific groups and individuals engaged and involved in using them. This distinction becomes quite clear when both groups of teachers are asked, "What is the very best thing that can happen to you as a teacher? What is hitting a home run for you?" Quitter/failures respond in the following way: "The best thing that could happen to me as a teacher would be if everyone in the class understood what I told them to do, did it correctly and passed in a correct, completed assignment. A home-run is when you don't have to go over the same thing again and again and still have some who don't get it and others who won't do it."

Stars answer the question this way: "The best thing that could happen to me as a teacher would be if I got everyone turned on and really involved in what they were doing. Hitting a home run is when the students at all levels are learning because they really want to." This difference between stars and quitter/failures in terms of what they think they are doing when they plan highlights the difference in their ideologies and in their teaching behaviors. In effect, while both groups all called "teachers" they are performing quite different jobs. Quitter/failures think they are engaged in acts of teaching regardless of how the children respond. These acts are outlined in Chapter VIII The Pedagogy of Poverty. Stars believe that no teaching can occur unless learning takes place. Stars' planning is primarily focused on how to interest and involve the students in seeing value in learning and becoming involved with the particular subject matter. Stars know that when they are able to motivate students that learning skyrockets and teaching becomes less stressful.

Differences in how these two groups of teachers plan is also manifested in terms of who they think their students are. Quitter/failures think in terms of one student. They prepare one lesson, one practice activity, one homework assignment. This is for the mythical average student in the classroom. If you ask them before they teach, "What have you prepared for the student who is three grades behind in basic skills?" Or, "What have you prepared for the inclusion students to do?" Or, "What have prepared for the student who finishes in half the time?" Or, "What have you prepared for the student who never passes in any work and just spends the period fooling around?" they have no answers to these questions. They simply do not plan anything for these students in spite of the fact they can accurately predict these students will not do the assignment they are planning and will cause trouble. It is irrational behavior to know in advance that the lessons they are planning will fail for half or more of the children but to not plan more than one activity for all the students. The explanation for this irrational behavior is that the ideology of these quitter/failures leads them to believe that 1) children who cannot do the work should not be in the classroom; 2) my job is to cover the required curriculum, if the children don't want to or can't learn the material it is their failure not mine; and 3) it is not possible to teach all the different levels of children they put in one classroom so that there is really nothing more I can do. Quitter/failures explain these three points repeatedly in their exit interviews.

The planning of stars reflects an ideology with the reverse assumptions. Since they can predict some students will not be able to do the work, several will not want to and others will be quick finishers in need of more work, they plan activities and make assignments that meet the various needs of all the children in their classrooms.

D. Coaching (You and Me Against the Material)

The way in which many teachers interact with their students results in an antagonistic relationship with the teacher and the subject matter to be learned on one side versus the students on the other. The process of learning, or more accurately not learning, becomes a process in which the teacher uses the particular subject matter to convince the student that s/he is incapable of ever learning it. The content areas in which this is most common are mathematics and science; however, it also occurs quite frequently in the teaching of grammar, foreign languages, music and swimming. In these and other subject matters many students bring baggage. Previous failures and negative experiences leave students with a fear of inadequacy. If the teacher moves ahead before these fears are allayed, the students become more concerned with avoiding failure than achieving…and the best way of avoiding failure is to stop trying.

Failure/quitter teachers use the material against the student when they show they are annoyed with students who are having difficulty. This happens when they find they must constantly correct students, or are forced to repeat something over and over. By demonstrating annoyance and frustration they send the message, "If you weren't so stupid I wouldn't have to constantly repeat and make endless corrections in your work." This frustration on the teacher's part is fully transmitted to the students. The drama being played out has a simple story line. The teacher is using the content to prove to the student that s/he is not capable of learning the particular material and in many cases that s/he is not capable of learning much at all. Without really being sensitive to the message they are transmitting to students, many teachers delude themselves into believing that they are really hard-working professionals and that the lack of student achievement is not really their fault. They make comments such as, "I have to move on. I can't keep repeating the same thing." The real problem here is even if the teacher repeated the lesson endlessly the student would not learn the material. A failed method of getting something across does not become a successful method by repeating it more slowly or louder. Professional intelligence is demonstrated by failing in new ways, not by repeating the same failed method again and again. Quitter/failure teachers do not have alternative lessons, or different examples, or more engaging materials for students having difficulty.

This process of battling the teacher and the material discourages learners. The fact that many children put themselves through this wringer daily for thirteen years of schooling is a greater source of wonderment than the smaller number who become troublemakers or disengaged.

Stars do the reverse. They show the students they are on the same side. The message their behavior sends to students is, "It's you and me against the material." They do this by coaching and providing endless encouragement. This is sophisticated and difficult teaching. It requires the teacher to put the content into small steps which lead the students from success to success. When the teacher shows the student, "We can do this together." They both derive a sense of efficacy and well-being. The student feels the power that comes from learning things that used to be difficult or impossible and the teacher derives the satisfaction that comes from creating situations in which the students succeed. Stars actually study their students' thinking processes to identify the particular ways of thinking that may be blocking their learning. They then coach individuals and small groups in overcoming these specific obstacles. They are not only expert in the subject matter but in how students think about the subject matter. Stars see themselves as coaches not as simply judgmental assessors. A coach constantly shows how in new and interesting ways. Coaching is the never ending process of convincing the learner, "You can do it. I know you can!" This convincing is not done by lecturing or giving pep talks but is accomplished by learning the students' thinking processes regarding the specific subject matter and providing lessons which alter the way the student processes that content. Stars define the problem of students having difficulty with the material by saying to themselves, "There's nothing you can do that will prevent me from coming up with better ways for you to learn this material."

E. Commitment to Students with Special Needs

In many urban school districts the number of special need students now exceeds twenty percent. In my city school district of 89,000 students there are 18,000 children already labeled. Given declining enrolment and the growing number of students in the pipeline waiting to be tested each year, by 2007, there will be over 20,000 children or approximately twenty-five percent who are labeled with some handicapping condition. Children of color are disproportionately represented among children labeled as special need students. In many states and school districts these percentages are even higher and soaring. In Massachusetts twenty-eight percent of the children of color are designated as having special needs. Nationally, in 2002, there were over 6.5 million children labeled as having special needs and the overwhelming majority of them were in the 120 largest urban school districts.

The disturbing thing about this population is not the children with clear physical handicaps who can be readily identified on valid, objective bases. The problem lies with the majority of this special needs population who are placed in vague, difficult-to-define categories such as emotionally disturbed, cognitively disabled, or learning disabled. Most of the children in these categories are African American and other children of color. A disproportionate number are males. It is clear that large numbers of teachers, who cannot relate to or deal with children of color, are referring them for psychological evaluations and the psychologists are concurring with the teachers making the referrals.

THE MID-RANGE FUNCTIONS OF STARS WHICH CANNOT
BE ASSESSED IN INTERVIEWS

The way this issue is typically dealt with in the media is that there is not enough money to serve all the children with special needs and that the special education laws are an unfunded federal mandate. The most critical issue, however, deals with who is being labeled, by whom and on what basis? In the 120 largest urban districts it is no longer unusual for one-fifth or more of the students to be assessed and labeled as having special needs. What would happen in a small town or suburb if the school authorities were to define one-fifth of the children in the community as abnormal in some way? Would the parents simply acquiesce and would the schools just move along with business as usual? I would predict that there would be a public outcry strong enough to change the school board, the superintendent and many of the staff, and the state authorities would be called in to take over the school district until it could be restructured. There would also be several lawsuits--and the school district would lose them. Why is it that in the large urban districts, dealing with parents of color many of whom are in poverty, that one-fifth of the students can be defined as having special needs and the issue raised is one of getting more resources not "Who says all these children are abnormal?"

In the urban districts the practice of inclusion places children identified as having special needs into regular classrooms. The practice of inclusion reveals a clear, observable distinction between stars and quitter/failures. Stars include, accept and work with inclusion students in the same way they work with all children. Quitter/failure teachers do not. Stars think of special needs as merely another form of individual difference and because they believe their job as teachers requires them to account for all students' individual differences they do not see inclusion students as presenting them with more problems than teaching any students. In my studies of teacher problems, teachers rated as satisfactory or higher do not cite inclusion students as among their most difficult teaching problems. Finally, stars do not lower their expectations regarding what special needs students can accomplish. Star teachers frequently challenge visitors to their primary classrooms to pick out the students with special needs. The reason this is difficult is that all the children are being held to the same high standards and doing the same assignments. Star middle teachers typically report that they have students with handicapping conditions scoring higher on achievement tests than many of their "regular" students.

STAR TEACHERS

Frequently, children labeled in primary grades are never reevaluated no matter how well they do subsequently. Star teachers frequently seek to get students who are achieving at reasonable or higher levels "unlabeled." This requires a great deal of paperwork and many meetings, but stars are willing to do the work.

Quitter/failure teachers see no reason to have children with special needs in their classes. They feel that they did not choose to become special education teachers, and therefore, resist accepting responsibility for including them. They do not see these children as an asset to life in the classroom but as a hindrance which intrudes on their covering the required curriculum. They hold low or no expectations for these children and live down to those expectations. Visiting their classrooms one sees children with special needs engaged in meaningless activities such as coloring or merely sitting. The operating norm is that if they do not disturb the teacher or bother other students they will be allowed to stay. There is no interaction with other students who adopt the teacher's belief that students with special needs are an intrusion which must simply be put up with. How teachers' respond to children with special needs and how they impact their learning clearly discriminates between stars and quitter/failures.

F. Interactions with Parents and Community

All teachers claim they want to involve parents. The distinctions lie in what the teachers specifically wants parents to do and why these behaviors are regarded as valuable. Quitter/failure teachers expect parents to do two things: punish children who are misbehaving in school and function as homework helpers. In my city there are 13,000 homeless children and countless others who have no place to do homework or no adults at home who are available to help. When I ask these teachers, "Do you know which children in your class have homes? Do you know which children have parents at home evenings? What exactly do you know about the home conditions of your children?" Inevitably, their answers reveal ignorance and surprise because they just assume what home conditions should be. Many parents work two jobs. If there are two adults in the home there might be three or even four jobs between them. In 2004, economists hailed the rise in the Dow Jones and announced that the recession was over but there were still over 11 million unemployed and the number was rising. In our major urban areas as many as twenty-five percent of the male population of African Americans between ages sixteen and twenty-five remain unemployed regardless of how economists characterize the economy. The general condition of the total economy and the indicators used to assess the nation's economic health never reflect the economic conditions of minority populations in our urban areas.

Quitter/failures are notoriously insensitive to the home lives of their students. They do not make home visits and when informed that stars routinely do so are shocked that there are teachers who believe home visits and relating to parents and caregivers is part of their job as teachers. The behavior of quitter/failures demonstrates louder than their words that they believe the following about the role of parents: 1) if teachers cannot get children to follow classroom rules parents should be informed and make them comply; 2) if teachers cannot get students to do homework parents should work with them and see that they do it; and 3) if children are behind in basic skills parents should tutor them at home. In effect, quitter/failures believe that all the teaching skills they lack, i.e. relating to children, motivating children and teaching children, must be performed by parents and caregivers. They believe that if parents and caregivers do not compensate for what the children are not learning in school then it is the parents who have failed in their duties and not the teachers who have demonstrated professional inadequacies.

Quitter/failures talk down to parents. They assume that know more than parents not only about schooling but about child rearing and life in general. The way they communicate with parents delivers a very clear message to parents that they are being patronized. It is curious and almost humorous. On the one hand quitter/failure teachers regard parents as inadequate and uneducated and on the other hand they expect them to teach all the skills at home that they, the professional educators, have failed to teach during the day.

Star teachers do not view parents as responsible for teaching all the things at home that they have failed to teach during the day. When asked "What do you want of parents?" stars do not suggest the typical functions: i.e. disciplining students who misbehave, helping with homework, serving as a classroom tutor, helping on field trips, volunteering as a classroom helper at parties and special events. Stars see parents and caregivers primarily as resources. First, they seek to learn as much as possible from parents about the students in order to use their interests and talents to engage them and make their school learning as relevant as possible. Second, they want the parents to encourage and reinforce positive behaviors. Whenever stars have something good to report about children they inform parents so that the children will be encouraged at home as well as in school. Stars know the fantastic effect on children who are experiencing learning and behavioral difficulties when they find out that the teacher has just had a personal or telephone conference with their parents—and reported only the positive things they are doing in school. Third, stars have three-way conferences with parents and students. As the teacher demonstrates respect for parents by listening to their ideas and suggestions, the students are encouraged to believe that the teacher thinks of them as equals. As parents observe the teacher listening to their child, they begin to believe that this person really does care about my child. Fourth, stars seek to involve parents in class activities so that something they know and can do is showcased. For example, parents are the best resource people when teachers do units on occupations and are called upon to explain to the class the nature of their particular work. Parents are the best resources when teachers are doing units in social studies and are called upon to describe life in a different country or state. Parents are the best resources when the class is studying various arts, crafts, music, constructing various things, practicing particular hobbies, cooking, sewing, raising a particular animal, or even describing a fire or other event in the neighborhood. Parents are ideal resource people to describe what they did while in the military during a particular war or peace-keeping activity. Stars consciously search out ways in which parents are presented as knowledgeable people who know and can do things that are worth learning. The positive effects on children of having their parents presented in these ways cannot be overstated. Stars are extremely sensitive in structuring such activities on a regular basis. This builds trust and a sense among parents and caregivers that they, the teachers and the children are all engaged in a truly cooperative enterprise. In response to such treatment parents who would not dream of setting foot in the school to listen to another set of complaints about their child from someone who doesn't know or care about them, start calling teachers at home and volunteering their participation in any way the teacher deems best.

THE MID-RANGE FUNCTIONS OF STARS WHICH CANNOT
BE ASSESSED IN INTERVIEWS

The very best way in which star teachers involve parents is by creating opportunities for them to participate in culminating activities. After the children complete a unit of study parents are invited to hear the results of what their children have learned. These units might be a science project, the publication of a class magazine, the presentation of a class play, a debate on a controversial topic or a forthcoming election, a tribute to a great folk hero, or any other important piece of learning. Star teachers give parents frequent opportunities to take pride in their children's learning and children the opportunity to showcase their accomplishments. These activities, which combine final student accomplishments with parental involvement, are "culminating activities" and represent the typical way in which star teachers conclude all units to demonstrate that important learning has taken place.

As with the other mid-range functions, the beliefs and behaviors of stars versus quitter/failures in terms of parental involvement clearly discriminates between the two groups. Quitter/failures want homework helpers and disciplinarians. Stars want genuine partners in their student's educations.

G. Creating Student Ownership

The message delivered to students by quitter/failures is "This is my room. I don't need you here. Unless you shape up you're out of here." The message delivered by stars is the reverse: "We need you. If you don't contribute we won't be able to make it without you." How do star teachers get a difficult message like this across after students are told again and again that it is the teacher's room and the teacher's work they are interrupting?

With the support of a National Education Defense Act grant, I spent a full year in an urban middle school identifying the behaviors of great urban teachers. As I proceeded with my work I was constantly interrupted by the "noise" from the music room across the hall. It took several months for me to realize that the "noise" was a volunteer choir of almost 100 youngsters under the direction of Mrs. Bissell the music teacher. It took several more months for me to realize that this choir included many youngsters who were causing trouble in the rooms of other teachers. It finally struck me that if Mrs. Bissell could get this large group of youngsters, who other teachers didn't want in their rooms, to voluntarily come during their lunch period when they could be outside the confines of the building, that there might be something going on here that I could learn from. Mrs. Bissell never had any discipline problems, never suspended anyone and did not seem to have the management problems that plagued the other teachers who dealt with these very same students. Perhaps Mrs. Bissell was an effective teacher? After I finally realized that Mrs. Bissell was doing more than generating "noise", I began to observe her teaching and question her in an effort to ferret out the reasons for her success. Her choirs were not only recognized citywide but were frequently recognized with music awards in statewide competitions.

First, I observed her several times. Mrs. Bissell followed no pedagogical method that could be discerned. Essentially what she did was stand at the piano and play while she shouted instructions: "You're late tenors!" "Faster!" "Louder!" This would go on for the period. The bell would ring and the students would leave. Next day the students would file in, sit down and Mrs. Bissell would announce the piece they were to sing then begin banging on the piano and shouting directions.

In questioning Mrs. Bissell, all of the traditional conceptions which purport to explain teaching effectiveness were shattered. Mrs. Bissell had no teacher education of any kind. She had been playing piano in a cocktail bar where the middle school principal would go for a drink after school. After the fourth music teacher quit, the principal approached Mrs. Bissell about teaching in the school on a provisional license. Her first questions were: "What is the pay?" and "What do I have to wear?" When the principal assured her that special dress was unnecessary she realized that the could save a substantial amount of money because there would be no need to dry clean all the dresses she needed in order to play in the cocktail bar. Aside from the questions of pay and dress Mrs. Bissell asked no further questions regarding what the position would involve. The second thing I learned was that Mrs. Bissell knew nothing about the youngsters in the chorus. She didn't know what other teachers said about the students and never read any permanent records. Indeed, she never spoke to other teachers since she spent her free periods conducting the volunteer chorus. Mrs. Bissell never spoke to parents or visited homes. She knew nothing about issues such as diversity, equity, or multiculturalism and cared even less. The only parents she met were those who came up to her after a performance to thank her for all she had done for their children. In one of our conversations we had the following exchange:

M.H.: "Do you derive satisfaction from seeing the youngsters progress with learning the music?"

Mrs. Bissell: "Heck no. I grit my teeth having to listen to all those mistakes and the way they murder the music!"

I then asked her about the relevance of the music she selected. There was no rap or rock or Latino music. She had the youngsters singing the scores of old shows that she liked such as "Music Man" which was set in turn-of-the-nineteenth-century Iowa. Mrs. Bissell had the students singing four part barbershop harmony. As far as I could determine Mrs. Bissell's entire curriculum consisted of picking music that was relevant to her not the students, then teaching it by banging on the piano and shouting instructions to youngsters she knew nothing about.

After several months I was ready to admit defeat. There was nothing about Mrs. Bissell personally or in her teaching behavior that could account for 100 diverse, young adolescents ages thirteen to fifteen voluntarily singing their hearts out for her without the least bit of boredom or disruptive behavior. Especially puzzling was the fact that the music was completely irrelevant to their interests and backgrounds. As I was passing her room one day she stopped banging on the piano and yelled across the room to a large young man sitting with his feet on a chair munching on a huge hero sandwich. (Since the youngsters all came during lunch hour eating was permitted.) Their dialogue was as follows:

Mrs. Bissell: "Louie you're not singing." (She stops banging on the piano. All eyes turn toward Louie. Louie is a gang leader with a reputation for not taking stuff from teachers.)

Louie: "I'm eatin' my sandwich." (Tension builds. The class waits.)

Mrs. Bissell: "You could hum. You know I need altos."

STAR TEACHERS

At this point Mrs. Bissell returned to banging on the piano, the chorus returned to their singing and Louie kept eating his sandwich…and humming. Mrs. Bissell performed one major function of star teachers and this one function was sufficiently powerful to not only compensate for all the things she didn't do but to make her an exceptionally effective teacher. She convinced the youngsters, "I need you. I can't do what we need to do here without you. You are not only important, you are everything!" Quitter/failures transmit a message to students that is the exact opposite. "I don't particularly want or need you here interrupting my work!" "It's my way or the highway."

Star teachers consciously and deliberately do what Mrs. Bissell did in all subject matters, not just in areas such as choral music which obviously depends on student participation. Their demeanor and behavior communicates to the students that, "This is your class, your work, your effort. Whatever happens here that's good and praiseworthy is something that you make happen. I need you and the class needs you. Without you we wouldn't have a project, a team, or an activity that can be fully completed." This message that the classroom and the activities belong to the students, not the teacher, is communicated by the manner in which the teacher speaks and demonstrates respect for students, never by preaching or lecturing. Star teachers work hard to think of, plan for and offer activities that lead the students to believe the work of the class is totally dependent on them. One of the indicators that such a student-centered climate has been created in a classroom is that even when youngsters are sick they still come to school. Star teachers have fantastic attendance. None of this will happen until and unless the teacher's ideology includes the belief that the class belongs to the students.

Chapter XIII
The Mid-Range Functions of Stars Which Can Be Assessed in Interviews

This chapter describes the seven mid-range functions of star teachers which can be discerned in personal interviews. To help the reader understand them I have included some dialogue along with the narrative description. The dialogues are snippets taken from more than 3,000 interviews. The dialogues reveal the thinking of stars and how their ideology differs from quitter/failures. The way stars think cannot be separated from their observable behaviors. Their actions reflect their ideology and vice versa. This ideology includes their beliefs about the role of the school serving diverse students in poverty, the nature of learning and the nature of teaching. Because one must have a strong commitment to this undergirding ideology it is not possible to translate what stars do into "ten easy steps" for anyone to follow. To do what stars do requires sharing the beliefs and values they use as guidelines for making the countless decisions they make daily. To try to imitate what stars do, without believing as they do, leads to merely going through the motions of teaching and having little influence on students' learning. For those who accept stars' ideology, these functions can be brought to life; they can become a source of insight and a guide to effective teaching.

H. Persistence

The first mid-range function performed by star teachers which can be assessed in a personal interview is sometimes referred to as problem solving. At times, it appears to be an indicator of creativity. Over the years I have come to regard it as persistence because it is inextricably linked to commitment. After listening to star teachers explain their work, I realized that this attribute does not reflect simple stick-to-itiveness. It refers to the deep and abiding beliefs that stars hold about the nature of diverse children in poverty; the nature of their potential; the nature of the teacher's role; and the reasons stars believe they and the children are in school. Each of these mid-range functions represents a cluster of teacher behaviors and the ideology stars hold for engaging in these behaviors. Thus, persistence represents both how stars act and what they believe.

As an ideology, persistence can best be described in the following manner. Stars believe that it is their responsibility to keep trying to find ways of engaging their students in learning. Stars describe their jobs—to themselves and to others—as the continuous generation and maintenance of student interest and involvement in learning. They manifest their ability to persist in several ways. First, for the class as a whole, they feel a constant responsibility to make the classroom an interesting, engaging climate which, on a daily basis, will involve all the children in meaningful learning activities. Second, on an individual level, stars are persistent in meeting the needs of everyone in the room: the talented, those with handicapping conditions and the frequently neglected "gray area" students. Stars verbalize their persistence like this: "There may be thirty kids in this class but if I find an especially vital activity for one or two children each day I can reach everyone on an individual basis several times every month." This view of their role as attempting to reach individuals requires great persistence. The third way in which stars demonstrate this attribute is with problem children. The ultimate test in teaching is finding "what works". This phrase is teacher talk for "Was the problem controlled?", or "Did the child with the problem stay on task and stop bothering others?" Searching for "what works" is a clear demonstration that stars believe that teaching is a craft devoted to managing symptoms not treating deep-seated causes of students' behavior. Whatever the reasons for children's behavior—whether personality, poverty, a handicapping condition, a dysfunctional home, or an abusive environment—star teachers take responsibility and accountability for managing children, seeing that they work cooperatively in a confined space for long periods and ensuring that they learn.

The following two conversations illustrate stars' persistence in thought and action. The first dialogue is with a low-potential teacher on the way to quitting or failing. In contrast, the second dialogue is with a star. In reading these it is important bear the attribute of persistence in mind.

THE MID-RANGE FUNCTIONS OF STARS WHICH CAN
BE ASSESSED IN INTERVIEWS

Conversation #1

Setting:	Third/fourth grade split
Problem:	Child who does not do homework
Questioner:	Imagine that when you start school next September you have a youngster who doesn't do his/her homework. Several days go by and this behavior continues. What might you do?
Teacher #1:	I'd find out why the child was not doing his homework. There could be many, many reasons. Some children don't do homework because they don't have a place to work. Others just lose stuff on the way home.
Questioner:	Jerome hasn't done his homework for several days. What might you do about this problem?
Teacher #1:	I'd try to find out why.
Questioner:	Would you talk to him?
Teacher #1:	Yes, I would talk to him.
Questioner:	Would you speak to him in front of the class or privately? What would you say to him?
Teacher #1:	I'd probably talk to him privately. I'd try to find out what was going on. Maybe offer to help him.
Questioner:	Suppose having this private conference works. Jerome brings in his homework for the next two days. On the third day there is no home work. What would you do now?
Teacher #1:	I'd talk to him again. Maybe try to encourage him with a reward of some sort.
Questioner:	Suppose that works and Jerome hands in homework for another few days but then he stops. What would you do then?
Teacher #1:	Well, after speaking to him several times I would mention some consequence if he doesn't do his homework.
Questioner:	Like what?
Teacher #1:	Oh, perhaps withdrawing a privilege—something he enjoys, like recess.
Questioner:	Now you've spoken with him several times and withdrawn some privileges. What might you do now?
Teacher #1:	By this time I would probably call a parent, perhaps discuss the situation with his mother.

Questioner: O.K. Let's imagine that this works too…but only for a few days. After two days Jerome is back to his old ways. No homework. What might you do now?

Teacher #1: Well by this time the problem has been going on for some time. I might take the matter up with the school psychologist and have Jerome tested. There might be something wrong with him.

Questioner: That may be true, but the school psychologist has a backlog of children who have been referred to him. It might take six months to test Jerome. Is there anything else you might do?

Teacher #1: At this point I might ask the principal for help. Maybe a three-way meeting with the mother.

Questioner: And Jerome?

Teacher #1: Maybe, sure.

Questioner: I realize you may be getting tired of this question, but I have to ask one more time. Jerome is still not handing in his homework. What might you do at this point?

Teacher #1: At this point it is clear that there is something seriously wrong with Jerome. I don't know. (Pause.) It's tough. (Pause.) I might ask to have Jerome put in another classroom.

Questioner: O.K. Let's pull away from Jerome and no homework. Let's look at the whole job of teaching this class. Think about all the teacher tasks: ask yourself the question, "I wonder what I might try next?"

Teacher #1: "I wonder what I might try next?"

Questioner: That's right but not in relation to a child with a problem but in relation to everything you have to do as a teacher.

Teacher #1: Well, I would guess a lot now that I think about it.

Questioner: Once a year, once a month, once a week, "I wonder what I might try next?"

Teacher #1: Well I think it's important to be well planned. If you are well-planned and there aren't any Jeromes…

Questioner: Assume things are going well. How often would you ask yourself that question?

Teacher #1: Oh, then I would guess it would not be so necessary. Maybe once every couple of weeks, maybe once a month. I'm not sure.

THE MID-RANGE FUNCTIONS OF STARS WHICH CAN
BE ASSESSED IN INTERVIEWS

The following conversation raises the same problem with a star teacher.

<u>Conversation #2</u>

Setting: Third/fourth grade split

Problem: Child who does not do homework

Questioner: Imagine that when you start school next September you have a youngster who doesn't do his homework. Several days go by and the behavior continues. What might you do?

Teacher #2: I probably wouldn't wait a couple of days.

Questioner: All right. Let's assume it was the first day. What would you do?

Teacher #2: I'd take the child aside privately and try to find out what the problem was. Did he understand the assignment? Did he want to do it? Why? Why not? Maybe there's some other problem that's getting in the way of his doing his homework.

Questioner: O.K. So you would speak with the child. Suppose that didn't work. What would you do now?

Teacher #2: I'd be likely to look for something that seemed to interest him and make up a special assignment for him.

Questioner: So you would give him something special to do?

Teacher #2: Something that I knew he could do and wanted to.

Questioner: O.K. Let's imagine that you went to all the trouble of making up a special assignment for him and he still didn't do it.

Teacher #2: Well, I would want to check out what might be preventing him.

Questioner: What would you do?

Teacher #2: Would it be all right if I gave you more than one answer at a time?

Questioner: Sure.

Teacher #2: I'd probably chat with the teachers who had him previously and see if s/he had this problem. I might ask another adult in the school to speak with him for the purpose of finding out what was going on that he was not telling me. Children of this age who know they've done some thing wrong are not always forthcoming. I might check the school records. I

135

might find out who in the class was his friend and see what they could tell me about his interests and talents. He might have a brother or a sister in another class who might be helpful. Perhaps a teaching assistant has worked with him in the past and could give me some insights. If the matter persisted over time I might make a home visit and find out how he spends his time.

Questioner: You've mentioned seven or eight things. I notice you haven't spoken with the school psychologist or the principal.

Teacher #2: I might speak with the principal, but I'm assuming that no homework is my problem, not a cause for suspension or something. I haven't spoken with the school psychologist for several reasons. First, they test then they say "This child could be helped by more individual attention." Heck, all children can be helped by more individual attention. Second, I'm not looking to have the child put in a special class because his crime is no homework. So far that's all you've said he's done—or not done.

Questioner: O.K. So now we have a bunch of things you would do and a few you would not do. The child is still not handing in any homework.

Teacher #2: I'd keep talking to him. I'd keep trying to find things he could do successfully without him having to take too many materials back and forth between home and school.

Questioner: You're back on the action you tried at the beginning.

Teacher #2: That's right. Talking with children is my job. So is trying to find things they can do and will do.

Questioner: You would do the same things that don't work over and over?

Teacher #2: They do work. I'm pretty sure this problem would have been solved a long time ago. You keep stating its not working. Children don't resist doing things they care about—particularly with other children and teachers who show an interest. That's another thing I would do. Create an expectation from myself and the other children in the class who are interested in learning that we all want to hear about the particular assignment this child has done for homework.

136

THE MID-RANGE FUNCTIONS OF STARS WHICH CAN
BE ASSESSED IN INTERVIEWS

Questioner: We've spent a lot of time on this...

Teacher #2: Don't be concerned. I will work it out with this student.

Questioner: O.K. Let's pull away from this homework issue. I'd like to get some overall sense from you about how often you would ask yourself the question, "I wonder what I might try next?"

Teacher #2: "I wonder what I might do next?"

Questioner: Yes, but not in relation to discipline or problems but in relation to your total work as a teacher...as you look at your total role in the classroom. Whether it's learning, managing, or whatever, how often would you ask yourself, "I wonder what I do next?"

Teacher #2: A lot would depend on the class.

Questioner: Let's assume things are going well and there are no serious problems.

Teacher #2: There are never "no problems", but whatever you mean I can tell you that I ask myself this question all the time.

Questioner: Once a month, once a week, once a day?

Teacher#2: All the time. Everyday. Countless times each day. Even when things seem to be going well the children could always be learning more. I could be finding more ways of involving them and eliciting greater activity and learning from them. Since I can never engage them enough in learning, I can never stop finding a better way. I can imagine asking a question like, "What do I do next?" for the class, for a group, for one child, twenty times a day.

As we contrast the answers of Teacher #1 and Teacher #2 several clear differences emerge. Teacher #1 perceives the problem as something that should not occur while Teacher #2 perceives the problem as part of her normal, expected workload. Teacher #1 perceives the problem as something that should be dealt with through a series of rewards and punishments. Teacher #2 does not define the issue as involving rewards and punishments but as her search for an activity that will gain the child's interest. Teacher #1 perceives of herself as the authority in search of the surefire method of forcing compliance. Teacher #2 perceives of her role less as an authority and more as a caring adult who is accountable for involving a child in learning. Teacher #1 seeks support from the principal and school psychologist. Teacher

#2 sees these individuals as being of little help in this situation—unless they happen to know the child personally and can offer some specific ways of involving him and this seems an unlikely possibility to Teacher #2. Teacher #1 sees relating to the parents as helping to enforce compliance. Teacher #2 is loathe to complain to the mother but would approach her to learn more about the student's interests; i.e. "is there something the child is interested in or good at?" Teacher #1 is in search of a final solution: either the child will comply or be taken out of the room. Teacher #2 sees the possibility that this issue will be ongoing. It may be solved temporarily, but it is likely to crop up again, with this child or another one. While Teacher #2 is very confident she will solve the problem she is open to the possibility that she may have to revisit the problem again and again in future. This doesn't seem to upset her since she defines her primary teaching task as finding things that will involve children in learning. The ideology Teacher #2 conveys—and it can be verbalized in various ways—is something like this: "If teaching were simply a question of giving children assignments and monitoring compliance then anyone could be a teacher. The knowledge we teachers need to bring into the classroom is how to elicit interest and engage youngsters in wanting to do the work of learning. It may seem harder, but I can tell you that working with volunteers is a lot easier than overseeing prisoners."

The second question: "How often do teachers ask themselves, 'What do I do next'" also highlights differences between the two teachers. Teacher #1 perceives the question to be reasonable only if there are problems. When the question was restated as, "In a class that's working well how often would you ask yourself this question?" she could not really see any sense in the question. This is because Teacher #1 does not define her role as one of constantly searching for more effective ways of involving children. Also, Teacher #1 does not define her job as an open-ended one in which the children can always do more and learn more. Teacher #1 sees teaching as essentially managing. Having no problems means that the students must all be complying and if this is the case then there is no need to be concerned about having to do anything better. Teacher #1's motto is "If it ain't broke don't fix it."

In contrast, Teacher #2's ideology leads her to believe that learning can always be increased. She sees endless potential for the children beyond compliance. She knows that all students can always be learning more. Teacher

#2 feels and acts accountable for involving the children more and more. Because she does not conceive of learning as a finite task she persists and persists and persists. Teacher #2 and the behavior of all stars, demonstrates that they perceive of persistence as their day-to-day work. They do not stop until they find meaningful work for every child. And if they should link every child in the classroom with a useful learning activity they will continue to persist by asking themselves, "Is this the very best activity that can be devised or might there be something even better for these students to be doing?" Stars think in terms of maximum not minimum standards.

For star teachers persistence is not merely a set of behaviors. It is also a clear reflection of what they believe the daily work of the teacher to be. The logs of Thomas Edison reveal that he made 10,000 trials before discovering the tungsten filament for the light bulb. Edison described his belief in persistence this way: "The difference between coal and diamonds is that diamonds stayed on the job longer."

I. Protection of Students' Learning

For star teachers the ultimate value to be preserved is learning. For quitter/failures it is order. Stars live out this commitment to learning by seeking out current events, questions, discrepant events, current crises and emergencies. They then bring these into the classroom as a way of engaging their students and going beyond the traditional text-based curricula. Stars' have two sources of interesting material. They stay alert and sensitive to current events that might capture the imagination of children. They also have their own interests and avocations which they bring in and share. Examples of the former might be short-term and one-time topics such as: a heroic dog has saved a child who has fallen into a river; a local resident has made a hit musical disc and become a celebrity; a controversy rages regarding the location of a chemical waste dump. The endless issues which surround the lives of children provide food for thought, analysis, discussion and problem solving. Children are readily involved in reading, writing, debating and thinking about the living issues that provide us with persisting life problems. Star teachers use these "hot topics" as vehicles for bringing to life concepts in science, math and social studies, and therefore, making them meaningful to children. Less able teachers "cover" topics by reading or talking about ideas as remote abstractions. Concepts required to be taught in the curriculum can be dealt with as largely irrelevant to the students' lives or they can be given personal meaning. Taught in personally meaningful ways, key concepts from all the disciplines of knowledge can be learned, remembered and used by even the youngest children. Unfortunately, teachers without sufficient content knowledge do not have a basis for knowing what to emphasize and what to skip. They are limited to only following the textbook page by page and cannot bring the subject matter to life. Stars use texts but texts use failure/quitter teachers.

What this means in practice is that what is discussed, experimented with, written about and read, i.e. the actual activities pursued in classrooms, is different in the rooms of stars than it is in the rooms of other teachers. In the rooms of failure/quitters there is a clear pattern of, "Take out your books and turn to page 58." Or, "It's 10:30 and time for science. Take out your books and read chapter three. Who hasn't read yet?" Or, "Open your American People text and turn to page 164. Yesterday we left the Pilgrims speaking to Squanto." What a classroom observer witnesses are rituals not learning behaviors: e.g. teachers and children reading a text and the teacher using a set of prepared questions from the teacher's guide…questions and answers that purport to be meaningful and relevant to all children everywhere! The most common ritual is having the children simply taking turns reading from the text. It is also a typical practice for children to read a section silently and then write out answers to the questions at the end of the chapter. The teacher then repeats the questions and calls on children to read the answers they have written. Sometimes there's a test and the children exchange papers or they pass them in for the teacher to grade. If the teacher has taken a workshop in "cooperative" learning she may divide the class into teams to answer the questions in the text. There is no attempt to make what is being covered relevant to children's lives or to make learning an active search rather than passive reading about things. If children spend five or six hours a day for thirteen years performing these rituals they emerge as semi-literate, largely ignorant, with no commitment to learning and no skills which will enable them to learn should they become interested in studying something in future.

Publishers sell textbooks as "programs" to school boards and administrators. They guarantee these "programs" as teacher-proof learning systems rather than just textbooks. In addition to the books themselves there are teacher guides, student work books, pictures, bibliography, a computer disk, supplementary materials and tests. Using these "programs" the teacher "covers" the required content. The whole package is premised and sold on the assumption that the teacher can be ignorant and disinterested in the content s/he is teaching, but by following the teacher's guide s/he will be able to effectively teach the material, even to reluctant learners. In several cities the teachers are required to give their lessons by reading a script printed in the teacher's guide.

Unfortunately, you can teach what you don't know and don't particularly care about. Teachers who don't know why it rains, or what causes summer, "cover" the science curriculum. Others who don't know how to divide fractions, or the causes of wars, "cover" math and social studies. Using their reading skills and staying a chapter, or even a page, ahead of the class, teachers who don't know what's in the Constitution "cover" good citizenship. Others who have never worked at a job other than teaching "cover" the skills students will need to get and keep a job, and to prepare for careers in the world of work. Such malpractice is also extended to newer parts of the curriculum such as multicultural education or the teaching of equity and justice issues. The teaching force is overwhelmingly white, female and monolingual and is comprised of individuals who work fifty miles from where they grew up and attended school. With little or no personal experience of living and working in a diverse society and with no theoretic or research knowledge base of American diversity, these teachers "cover" the curricula espoused by liberal educators just as superficially as they "cover" the traditional curricula. The oft-quoted aphorism, "You can't teach what you don't know" is only the first half of this famous admonition. The rest of the quote is just as important and adds: "about places you ain't never been." If the teacher is not an avid reader how can s/he teach others to see the joys and values of reading? If the teacher does not vote or participate actively in community affairs how can s/he teach citizenship? If the teacher has never worked at a job in which the employees are held accountable, where employees are not "entitled" to a given number of sick days and from which employees can be fired with no notice, how can s/he teach others to cope with the stress of making it in the private sector? The answer is always the same: teachers without the knowledge and experience base do not actually teach the material in the curriculum, they "cover" it.

This might appear to be the age-old liberal arts criticism of teachers and teacher education, but it is infinitely more complex. The reason we can no longer abide teacher ignorance relates most directly to equalizing educational opportunity for diverse children in poverty. The best way to define educational disadvantage is to think of it in the following way. To the extent that a child is dependent on schools and teachers for what s/he learns, that child is educationally disadvantaged. The child who shows up in kindergarten already knowing how to read and count is considered "ready" to learn by the teacher. The teacher doesn't think it is her responsibility to teach all the children these things. She assesses and sorts and is not held accountable for teaching all the children these things. She only wants children who demonstrate "readiness" by already knowing what she should ostensibly be teaching. As the children get to higher grades, teachers want students who already have all the prerequisite skills and who only need one explanation of any new material they "cover". Students who don't get it from one-time, one size-fits-all explanations are defined as students who are not "ready" for that grade and who shouldn't be there. In such a system children who are dependent on teachers for what they learn are clearly "disadvantaged."

Children in poverty and from diverse cultures are less likely to have the life experiences, the language, or the adult models from whom to learn what schools expect them to know to be considered "ready" by teachers who "cover" material rather than teach it. Children in poverty are less likely to grow up amidst, pharmacists, writers, environmentalists and others who can serve as knowledgeable people who are not only successful professionals but who derive a great sense of well-being from being life-long learners of various disciplines. I am not referring here to only knowledgeable people in the traditional professions but to the daily experience of interacting with adults who study and learn because they are enthusiastic students of subjects from which they derive personal benefits, not necessarily monetary or tangible ones. These are people who are intrinsically motivated to be lifelong learners and who need no intrinsic rewards to continue learning more about music, botany, philately, car repair, computer technology, or breeding dogs. Children in poverty have significantly fewer first-hand, in-depth contact with such models of learning.

THE MID-RANGE FUNCTIONS OF STARS WHICH CAN
BE ASSESSED IN INTERVIEWS

Why is this important? What does it have to do creating intrinsic motivation among children in poverty? Everything! Teachers who try to motivate children by telling them about the future are dead in the water as generators of interest. They say things like, "You will need to know this someday to fill out an application to get a job." Teachers who pursue this method end up repeating the same, stale, extrinsic reasons for learning literally thousands of discrete lessons. It does not work because it is a meaningless, untrue promise. Neither young children nor adolescents are turned on to learning by notions of future employment. If all the people in poverty woke up tomorrow being able to read on grade level there would still not be enough good jobs to go around. From knowing the state of their communities and their families, even young children intuitively know that such promises are apocryphal. The teachers know very well that using the promise of a future job cannot be used to justify learning about Andrew Jackson, the rivers of the American west, or distinctions in usage between that and which. Teachers' exhortations about future jobs cannot justify all the things that children should learn in school. Such reasons cut no ice with children and youth who are focused on neither the past nor the future but on the present. In contrast, stars' ideology is that schooling is not just preparation for living but for living now. Their ideology fits well with children's developmental need to see immediate uses and applications for what they are learning.

Where does this leave us? If their daily lessons cannot be rationalized in terms of a future job (and staying out of jail) how are teachers to interest and engage students in learning? Stars believe that their best hope is to imbue the lessons and activities offered to children with intrinsic value. They know that children can be naturally turned on to learning because learning is a natural human need. Children begin school as avid learners before they are turned off. Paul Torrence's studies of human creativity found that children at aged five were in the 90th percentile or higher on every test he used to measure creativity. At age fifteen, he found that children were in the 10th percentile or lower on these same measures. What happens to children between the ages of five and fifteen that turns them from being the most creative searchers for knowledge, to the least curious and most stereotypic in their thinking? Children begin school in love with learning. As kindergartners there is little they enjoy more than learning stuff. They begin knowing the joys of learning and they readily express and share these feelings. By high school the teacher's biggest complaint is student apathy. What has happened to squelch the intrinsic motivation for learning that is typical of young children? Clearly the explanation lies in what has happened to them in schools. Stars believe that with persistent effort they can protect the natural interests students demonstrated as preschoolers, when they enjoyed learning for its intrinsic value.

How do stars get beyond the teacher having to pretend that everything learned in school must be justified by connecting it to someday performing a job? How do they get students to buy into the notion that "We do this because we can learn a great many new things?" In truth, stars are seldom if ever nagged by students with, "Why do we have to be learning this particular topic or subject?" The ideology of stars supports the belief that the role of the school is broader than job training, that there will be some things that may not be fun or easy to learn and that gaining new ideas, skills and concepts is of intrinsic worth. Stars communicate this ideology to their students by involving them in the planning, execution and evaluation of everything that goes on in the classroom. On a daily and long-term basis, stars' students have an important voice in planning what and how they are taught. This process convinces students that they have a voice, and that their interests are valued. To achieve such student buy-in stars seek to connect the mandated curriculum to students' interests and the persistent problems of living that they face. This requires more teaching skill than following a teacher's guide, greater knowledge of the students' lives than simply pretending that every lesson or piece of content will be needed for future employment, and sufficient knowledge of the content to know the difference between key concepts and trivia. In addition to trying to make learning relevant by connecting it to students' lives and interests, stars do something else that is extremely powerful. They model their own intrinsic interest in learning. In the presence of their students, stars share things from books they are reading, write stories, compose pictures, build things, conduct experiments and engage in the full range of learning behaviors they expect the students to demonstrate. They frequently share their hobbies, music and pastimes including trips they have taken. A star's students see their teacher as someone who values learning and as someone who enriches her life by constantly learning new concepts and skills even though s/he is an adult and a teacher and no one is forcing her. By relating to their teacher through rapport caring and mutual respect, children are naturally drawn to explore and sample the teacher's interests and pursuits. And in those cases where the children can share the teacher's interests, there is a happy and productive relationship. But even in instances in which the youngsters do not come to share the teacher's particular interests, the teacher has still exerted a profound and salutary influence on the students. S/he has demonstrated and modeled the behaviors of an intrinsically motivated learner. Even the children who do not come to share the teacher's particular passion (e.g. Russian opera) are still shown and taught by example the value of developing their own interests and studies. Only learners can develop learners. This modeling dynamic is the reason it is vital for elementary, as well as secondary teachers, to not only be knowledgeable in the subjects they teach, but to demonstrate the joys which accrue from learning. Intrinsic motivation can only be modeled by those who are so motivated. Since values are caught not taught, star teachers' modeling is the primary means they use to teach their students commitment to learning. One never hears stars denigrate the value of what they are teaching with, "You'll need this for a job someday." Before our prejudices narrowed down the public school curriculum for diverse children in poverty to "get a job and stay out of jail", the stated curricula of the public schools was very close to the general liberal studies of university curricula. The curriculum included a range of social sciences, physical sciences, arts and humanities. And as in the general liberal studies in the university, the primary purpose of learning these disciplines, at any level, is not vocational but to enhance the individual and through him/her, the society at large.

Thus far, I have described modeling as the best way to rekindle and foster children's intrinsic need to learn and that using immediate, extrinsic rewards (or promises of future payoffs) will not be effective in creating lifelong learners. There is another critical dimension that distinguishes stars' ideology and functioning from other teachers. Stars' ultimate goal is for the children to transcend and surpass what their teachers know and are able to do. As a result, when stars "hook" their students into pursuing subjects and activities in depth, they have done the teacher's equivalent of hitting a home run. In contrast, quitter/failure teachers define the maintenance of order and having children who will follow their directions as hitting a home run. This difference in perception regarding the best thing that could happen to them as teachers is a major distinction between the ideology of stars and quitter/failures.

STAR TEACHERS

Star teachers find projects that interest children. They then plan with the children how they will set about studying these topics. Usually the projects are built around a set of questions or problems that are of vital interest to the children, but the teacher also understands how pursuing those interests will also facilitate the learning of the major concepts in the required curriculum. Star teachers draw upon their expertise and interests into fashioning class projects that students care about and which involve learning basic concepts and skills from the required subject matters. Following are just a few examples of how stars accomplish this by using the project method and thematic teaching.

1. A third grade teacher with some craft skills shares some of the musical instruments she has made with children in her previous classes. The teacher uses this to motivate the class to want to make their own instruments. Some turn out to be shaking instruments with different kinds of objects in different kinds of containers that make distinctive sounds when shook. Others are stringed instruments of different shapes and sizes with different numbers of strings of varying lengths; some are plucked and others require a bow. Many of the instruments must be struck together or hit with an object or with a hand. No two instruments are alike. All represent the individuality of their creators. None sound or looks like any traditional musical instrument. The construction takes over a month and requires the class to use math skills as well as arts and craft skills. Once built, the teacher has each child explain his/her instrument and how to play it. Children take turns playing their own instruments and those built by others. The teacher then has the children write stories and poems. Each child reads and explains his/her piece of writing to the class and the mood and feeling s/he is trying to convey. The children are then taught some basic skills of conducting an orchestra to get it to go fast/slow or loud/soft. Every child has an opportunity to conduct the orchestra as it plays background music to accompany the reading of his/her story or poem. The culminating activity is a performance in the symphony hall attended by parents and members of the symphony orchestra.

2. A teacher with an interest in gardening regularly brings plants into the classroom. Soon the room is not big enough to hold them and the class is given a plot that is part of an urban garden in what was formerly a vacant lot near the school. The children become interested in growing vegetables and in the problem of protecting their plot from neighborhood animals and

vandals. Many of the vegetables the children choose to grow are favorites of Asian Americans and African Americans and require a longer growing season. This means that seedlings must be started in the classroom in spring and tended in the outdoor garden over the summer. Volunteer gardeners are needed. The teacher and children also grow many plants started in the classroom in their home gardens. Parents become involved. While botany is the main study, children learn about weather, urban pollution and lead in the soil. The project leads to subsequent investigations of urban health hazards, nutrition and health.

3. A middle school teacher with knowledge and interest in physiology secures an old lie detector at a public auction. This device assesses an individual's veracity by measuring perspiration on the surface of the skin. The children become enthralled by this process for assessing lying. They speak and write endless scenarios as they take turns trying to beat the machine and lie without being detected. In addition to enhancing their speaking, writing and thinking skills, the teacher and children become fascinated with the question of why people perspire when they lie. Several students start dealing with concepts of scientific research. When a child fools the machine they demand, "Make him do it again!"(reliability). Other children raise the issue of how we can really be certain that an individual is sweating because he is lying and not because he is hot, overweight or exerting him/herself (validity). The activity also leads to a further study of why people lie and whether there are ever any good lies. The teacher's interest and knowledge of physiology encourages these studies. Her enthusiasm for learning along with the children serves as a model of the intrinsic learner.

4. A teacher with interests in foreign affairs and anthropology brings a short wave radio to class. The children begin listening to foreign broadcasts. The teacher picks up news in English, music and even some children's programming. The children become interested in the English-language broadcasts originating from all of the continents and even from remote places around the world. They begin a project on the different ways people speak English. They become more sensitive not only to international differences but to the differences represented by the diverse backgrounds in the classroom. Using the radio broadcasts and themselves as examples, they begin to collect and compile a computer program of the various ways

different people say the same things. Standard forms, vernacular, different usages, and Black English become continuous sources for comparison and learning. The project culminates with a series of stories and poems from a variety of English-speaking sources where English is the first, second or even third language used. The children not only improve their standard English but engage in genuine linguistic analyses by comparing different culture groups. These and numerous other examples can be gleaned from stars' teaching. They are themselves avid learners who bring some form of expertise to their work and then model their love of learning for the children. By modeling such involvement with learning, the teacher makes intrinsic learning a reality in the lives of the children.

Why should this discussion elaborating the need to have knowledgeable life-long learners as teachers be included in a section titled, "Protecting Learners and Learning?" This brings us back to this mid-range function of protecting students' learning, which can only be described once the teacher has been established as a life-long learner of something.

Star teachers achieve real learning in low-income schools by the project method and thematic teaching described in the four preceding examples. These examples are truly countless and are now readily available on the internet. Stars develop such projects throughout their careers. But here the explanation takes a confrontational turn since engaging students in learning can appear to pit the required curriculum against developing students as intrinsic learners.

Typical schools are not conducive to the project method described here. Schools are usually organized to meet state and district mandates that discrete subjects be taught for a certain number of minutes per day each week to children in the various grade levels. Where states do not have such narrow, prescriptive regulations, local school systems do. This rigidity is intensified by the practice of requiring specific texts for each subject at every grade level and expecting teachers to "cover" them. It is exacerbated by the alignment of the texts with mandated test. Many districts also require the teachers to use only direct instruction which is based on the assumption that "these" children can only learn by following directions and receiving extrinsic rewards. As a result of the culture that these conditions create, star teachers are quite likely to be regarded by principals and other teachers as working outside the proscribed curriculum. Indeed, this is typically true. Stars constantly report that their day-to-day teaching is frequently questioned and even resented by other teachers, or expressly forbidden by school administrators. Stars explain, at great length and in exhaustive detail, the strategies they employ to retain their freedom to teach using the project method and thematic teaching. In most cases, their teaching colleagues come to feel less threatened when they realize that stars only want to be left alone and not necessarily make others teach the way do. Many teachers are ill-equipped to offer anything but direct instruction because they are not lifelong learners committed to learning anything they can share with children. Stars must convince their colleagues that they will not be shown up or threatened in any way if they allow them the freedom to teach using the project method. This is not easy to do. If stars have children working hard and experiencing the joys of learning while other teachers cannot get these very same children to stay on task no matter how much they are bribed with extrinsic rewards, it is inevitable that other teachers will resent stars. If poor teachers are failing and under stress, they want all the other teachers working with the very same children to also be failing and under stress.

Stars must also cope with principals by convincing them that their children's test scores will not go down and will, indeed increase. They must also convince their principals that the benefits of the project method and thematic teaching are worth the extra field trips, the additional equipment, the unusual materials, the use of resource people, and the noise created by productive children at work.

It is no accident that stars generally have special agreements with school janitors. Their use of space, their need for extra equipment and their inevitably greater production of refuse require janitors to do more work cleaning up their classrooms.

The way this mid-range function plays out for many stars is as follows: "After I turn the class on to learning X, Y or Z, how do I protect them from the rigidities of the system?" The thematic units that stars use to engage students in learning are frequently perceived by rigid supervisors and administrators as activities that must be stopped. (The four examples above are mild deviations from the curriculum in comparison to others undertaken by stars and their children.) It is not unusual for these projects to conflict with school rules, bus schedules, or the use of space or equipment shared with other teachers. Frequently other teachers feel upstaged and threatened by stars' projects and complain about them to the principal, "If we have to follow the curriculum why doesn't she?" "Why can't she just teach like everyone else?" "I'm fed up with students complaining to me, 'that isn't the way we do it in her room'."

For these and other perceived abuses, stars are frequently prevented from pursuing projects. Sometimes this is a direct request from the principal; "I don't want you doing X, Y, or Z." Such directives are most common in the case of younger stars or newer principals. Frequently the desist orders are more indirect; e.g. "The school rules do not permit that activity." Or, "the curriculum requires a certain number of minutes per week be devoted to the various subjects and this activity is preventing that from happening?" Or, "the school's insurance doesn't cover that activity." In one way or another, stars must frequently choose between an activity that their children really enjoy and are learning from, versus complying with some school authority seeking to prevent the activity from proceeding. Stars always choose the children over the system. First, they try negotiating and reasoning, then proving that their children are learning the required curriculum but in a different way. They create portfolios. They invite skeptical principals and others to visit their classrooms. They willingly submit to having their children tested to demonstrate that they are achieving as much or more than children being taught by traditional instruction and textbooks. Stars frequently try to negotiate by moving some of the students' work time to before or after school, free time, weekends, or vacation periods. What they are not willing to compromise is the learning of children. Because the stars' primary goal is to find projects that engage their children in real learning, they are unwilling to simply give up these powerful learning activities because colleagues or superiors don't appreciate them, or find them inconvenient to have around. At the same time, stars are not confrontational. They seek to negotiate with a principal or others who try to shut down one of their projects. They are unlikely to escalate differences, start legal actions, or initiate union grievances.

THE MID-RANGE FUNCTIONS OF STARS WHICH CAN
BE ASSESSED IN INTERVIEWS

Consider the following incident: A star teacher's class is engaged in a project in which the students are vitally interested. The principal objects to the project. The objection is based on the belief that the teacher is not covering the material in the required curriculum. Also, the principal does not like the extra noise, equipment, cleanup, or smells emanating from the teacher's classroom. The principal tells the star to stop the project and go back to the regular curriculum, i.e. to use direct instruction and "cover" the required text according to the standard timetable. At this point the issue is clear: a genuinely engaging activity that is turning the students on to learning and raising their achievement vs. compliance with the school rules, policies, or a principal's directive. Quitter/failure teachers do not regard this as a dilemma. In the unlikely event they are accused of conducting such a project they would immediately desist. They explain this behavior by saying, "the principal runs the school." Or, "the principal is the boss." When informed that the children are really turned on to learning and love the project, they typically respond: "I'm not about to get fired." Or, "the principal is accountable for what happens in the school." A few quitter/failures go to the other extreme and become confrontational: "No one is going to tell me what to do!" Or, "I would take that to the union (superintendent) (parents) (school board)!"

Stars have two clear goals and stick to them. First, if the children are deeply involved in a valuable learning activity it is the teacher's responsibility to do whatever is reasonable to keep it going. Second, it is their job to patiently, courteously and professionally persist and negotiate with the principal. In contrast, quitter/failures offer quick and extreme solutions. Either they drop the project at the principal's first request, or they escalate the issue into a confrontation. On the other hand, when stars are faced with a request to stop an activity that has turned the children on, they engage in activities such as the following: have a conference with the principal; explain the project; ask the principal to visit the classroom; have a follow-up meeting with the principal; collect data to show that the children are learning as much and more than if the traditional methods were followed; collect samples of the children's work; have teachers and children from other classes learn about and observe the project; prepare a presentation (e.g. play, videotape, book, experiment, musical) that explains what the children are learning; keep talking with the principal.

STAR TEACHERS

Star teachers perceive of themselves as the grease between the children and any school rule or policy that would grind them down. In the final analysis, if stars are directly ordered to stop a project that they believe is turning on their students they would still figure out a way to offer it before or after school, or on their own time. Stars would never give up an activity that excites children and leads to genuine learning.

Interestingly, when asked "What would you tell the children if you stopped a project they cared about?" Quitter/failures respond that they would tell the children that it is the principal who is making them stop. The very teachers who obey the principal's orders are inevitably the ones who would lay the blame on him/her. Stars on the other hand, who might be negotiating persistently with a principal over several months in an effort to change his mind, would never tell their students that it is the principal who is trying to stop their project. Stars do not want the principal to lose status or stature in the eyes of the students. They are willing to take the heat for a decision they are fighting against. Stars want their students to see them as decision makers and not merely as people who must follow orders.

This is a critical point especially in a school serving low-income students. These children and their families are constantly abused or mistreated by bureaucracies such as the welfare department, health providers, housing authorities, insurance companies, the criminal justice system, utilities, etc. School is the only hope children in poverty have to experience a better life. They do not need to learn that schools are just another bureaucracy that only claims to be helping them but are really run for the benefit and convenience of those employed in them.

For children in poverty succeeding in school is a matter of life and death. They cannot all be rock stars and sports figures. They must make it in school or spend their lives in hopelessness and desperation. Children in poverty have no family resources, networks or safety nets to help them start careers or businesses. In order to have any hope of an occupation that will provide a living wage, health insurance and a place to live that is safe, they must succeed in school. For this reason educators cannot allow poverty students to believe that school is just like all the other bureaucracies in their lives; a place where much is promised but never delivered. Stars are sensitive to these conditions of life among their students. They know that once the students trust them and take the plunge into learning that those learning opportunities must be continued and not snatched back. As a result, stars protect the very principal who may be giving them a hard time or the school rules they don't agree with, even though these are very hard things to do. They know they must get their students to believe in and trust the value of education even if there are things about the particular school that don't work or which intrude on their learning. Stars also know that everything in school impacts the students; they learn from the informal and implicit curriculum as much or more than they learn from the formal one. As a result, if stars are forced to stop a project that students like, they take personal responsibility for the decision and plan new ways to engage the students. Stars are more concerned that the students do not lose faith in the school than they are in having to take responsibility for a principal's bad decision.

Quitter/failures are sensitive to none of this. Not having even thought about this they assume that the goal of the school for diverse children in poverty is limited to basic skills. Since they use the pedagogy of poverty or only direct instruction, they do not encounter the problem presented here. In the event the problem did arise they would immediately follow the principal's directive to desist and inform the students that it is the principal who is making them stop an activity they enjoy and are learning from. Because quitter/failures are insensitive to the need for helping children in poverty build trust in the value of schooling, they would not even consider the implications of these actions. If asked directly, "Would you tell the children the principal is making you stop an activity the students are enjoying?" they most frequently respond, "Of course. I always tell the truth."

This section might have been titled, "Response to Authority" instead of "Protecting Learners and Learning". To the uninitiated the problems presented here might refer to situations teachers rarely encounter, and therefore, are of little importance. That is precisely the point. The teacher who is less likely to be engaged in a project that is objectionable to administrators or other teachers is also less likely to be engaging students in vital learning activities. There are teachers who complete a career of thirty years without ever once being faced with the dilemma of continuing a learning activity that others object to. Stars, on the other hand, face this forced choice continuously throughout their careers. Their commitment to children's learning makes it inevitable that someone will be miffed, put out, or simply threatened by the effectiveness of their teaching. This becomes even truer in buildings officially designated as failing where the teachers and principal are under great stress. The presence of a successful, happy teacher and class in their midst is a clear indicator of their professional inadequacies. Rather than improve and change themselves, the inadequate unite to stamp out effectiveness. This dynamic helps to explain the downward spiral of urban schools over the last half century. Urban schools do change in significant ways: they get worse. Stars face this problem with persistence and good humor. Indeed, they are notorious for befriending their critics. Quitter/failures often claim, "I left because they wouldn't let me do X, Y or Z", when in reality they tried little out of the ordinary. Stars say, "They made me stop X, Y or Z, but I just moved on to J, K, and L."

J. Putting Theory into Practice

Poor teachers may perform a few best practices, but are unable to explain why they do what they do. Others are able to conceptualize and explain best practices, but are unable to manage a real classroom. Stars are able to do both. They organize and manage classrooms in which children are busy in constructive ways and can also explain the purposes of the activities, the nature of the learners and the principles of learning on which their methods are based. Quitter/failures are unable to demonstrate both the behaviors of competence and a grasp of their theoretic/research underpinnings. Some may appear to be getting things done in classrooms but can't justify why they are doing what they are doing. I call them "chargers". Others can justify classroom activities but cannot accomplish anything in their classrooms. I refer to them as "hesitant". This mid-range function refers to the teacher's propensity to connect theory to practice and vice versa.

The importance and relevance of this mid-range function is that it predicts the value teachers will derive from their future inservice activities. Teachers need to grow throughout their professional careers. They do this by connecting ideas with action and action with ideas. If individuals cannot make these connections they will have one year of experience thirty times rather than thirty years of experience. Theories and research findings from inservice

154

courses, principles learned in workshops, and the various ideas teachers get online, read or hear about, must all be translated into practice. In order for this translation to occur teachers must see the action implications of abstract ideas and ideals. The ability to transform an abstract generalization into a specific set of classroom activities for children is a vital function performed by stars. Without this ability to move between theory and practice, all forms of teacher education and professional staff development become a waste of time.

Stars are able to describe a large number of specific things they do to combine or synthesize discrete behaviors into an abstract principle or guideline for their instruction. If given a broad principal, e.g. "high teacher expectations lead to greater student achievement" stars are able to come up with a great number of specific behaviors—for themselves and the children—which demonstrate how this idea is implemented in the classroom. If we were to reverse the process and present them with a number of teacher actions, stars would be able to state the principles which support those actions. This ability to move from ideas to action, and action back to ideas, means that stars have the basis for continued growth throughout their careers. Without this predisposition and the ideology that self improvement is vital, quitter/failures lack the ability and motivation to reflect on their behavior and engage in anything other than rote learning, i.e. replicate with children the exact things they were taught during a particular inservice session. Stars willingness to reflect on their experience, i.e. "What is happening here? What I am learning from this experience?" "What might I do next time?" combines with their ability to relate ideas to action and forms the basis for the prediction that they will continue to grow on a career-long basis.

When teachers are asked, "Can you give an example of something that good teachers believe?" the most frequent responses are: "Good teachers believe all children can learn." "Good teachers have high expectations." "Good teachers know a lot about the children." "Good teachers involve the children in active learning." (The most common generalization made by those outside of education is, "Good teachers know their subject matter.") It would seem that there would be endless generalizations that might readily be made. This is not the case. There are many teachers and would-be teachers, who cannot respond to this question at all! Their thinking is so concrete that they can only report specific things that they do or that they have seen other teachers do, but are unable to state any generalization about what these specific behaviors add up to. In effect, they cannot finish the sentence, "Learning is most likely to occur when..." Some who can't respond to this question do not believe they should respond. Their position is that it is not possible to generalize about teacher behavior because generalizations are not always true, and therefore, making generalizations about teaching is the same as stereotyping. Others will not answer this question because they are convinced that one can only learn by experience and one person can never speak for another. This is an especially interesting point of view when held by teachers who spend most of their time teaching reading or other subject matters using reading. If experience is the best way to learn every form or knowledge why bother teaching children to read? In any event, there is a substantial number of college graduates who state straightforwardly that they "can only speak from personal experience" about any issue or topic and who regard the willingness to generalize as useless, even dangerous.

Actually, what scholars call knowledge are generalizations grouped into various disciplines of study. In researching this issue I have asked individuals who state that they can only be certain about things they have personally experienced, questions such as, "Do you believe WW II happened?" Or, "Do you believe a man really landed on the moon or was it a televised set up?" I have received responses such as, "Now that I think about it I really can't be certain. I certainly don't believe everything I read or see on television." These responses indicate that personal experience is the only basis many people use for determining what's true. In sum, the four reasons some people can't or won't use generalizations are: 1) they are concrete thinkers who simply don't think beyond the specifics of here and now; 2) they regard it as a dangerous practice because there are exceptions to any generalization; 3) they believe that making generalizations is the same as stereotyping; and 4) they don't really trust the validity of any way of knowing except personal experience.

These are interesting views when held by college graduates and teachers. What we call knowledge in the university consists essentially of generalizations grouped into departmentalized studies of history, mathematics, chemistry, literature, language, etc. These disciplines are all subject to change (knowledge generation) and are comprised of theories, propositions, concepts that are held to be generally true, not always true. For teachers to believe that a generalization must always be true in order to be valid would require us to deny that water freezes at 32 degrees Fahrenheit or that it snows at the North Pole, since there are instances when those things don't happen. Such notions reflect the thinking of those who have not derived much benefit from their university studies. Individuals, who do not believe that it is possible to make generalizations about teaching and learning because it is not possible to generalize about anything, have difficulty processing ideas. Consider the following dialogue with such an individual:

Questioner: Does smoking cause lung cancer?
Respondent: Yes.
Questioner: Suppose I told you that 60% of the people who smoke never get lung cancer.
Respondent: Well then it doesn't. It's an individual matter. A lot of smokers don't die.
Questioner: So then it wouldn't be a valid statement to say, "Smoking causes lung cancer.
Respondent: Not if so many people never die.
Questioner: Does drinking alcohol cause road fatalities?
Respondent: Yes.
Questioner: Suppose I told you that over 99% of the people who regularly drink and drive are never involved in a road fatality.
Respondent: Then it's like I say. It's not always true. You can't generalize.

The concept that generalizations are useful but merely vary in the degree to which they are valid is rejected as a way of thinking by such individuals. Many college graduates, including many teachers, do not have the ability to deal with gradations of meaning. It seems beyond their ability to process the concept that phenomena can be valid at various levels. The issue of the degree to which concepts are true becomes confused in their minds because they can only comprehend the word "true" as absolute. If something is true it is always true, as in religious truth. These people are dangerous to have as teachers of children since they have no understanding of the nature of knowledge. The fact that many of the teachers who are limited in this way are also concrete thinkers is not coincidental. Such teachers are not able to teach important knowledge but only information…and there is even a

STAR TEACHERS

problem with their ability to limit their teaching to information. For example, Washington D.C. is the nation's capitol…but it wasn't always the capitol. Two plus two is four…but not in base three. Children need teachers who can teach them the major ideas from the basic disciplines of knowledge as well as factual information.

Star teachers not only hold many generalizations about what constitutes good teaching and learning but can state the behavioral manifestations of these generalizations. Following is a dialogue with a star teacher on this issue.

Questioner: Please give a generalization you would make about good teaching.

Respondent: Good teachers hold high expectations.

Questioner: What might I see you doing in your classroom that would lead me to infer that you have high expectations?

Respondent: I wouldn't be ignoring pupils who are quiet and who might slip by unnoticed.

Questioner: What would you do that we might actually see that would lead us believe you hold high expectations?

Respondent: I might give some children a special assignment, or make sure to include them in the discussion, or maybe simply stand near them. These are ways of showing them I expect them to perform.

Questioner: How else are high expectations demonstrated?

Respondent: Lots of ways. If a child answers an open-ended question with one word, or says, "I don't know." or remains quiet, you have to do something to show them you believe s/he can do it. I would wait, take time to listen, provide encouragement.

Questioner: Are there any other ways?

Respondent: Sure. Some children frequently need extra assignments and harder tasks. The children have to see that you are involved emotionally— that you care how well and how much they do. This shows them that you believe in their ability and hold high goals for them.

Questioner: How do you demonstrate this caring?

Respondent: I demonstrate that I care by preparing lots of extra things they

158

	might do. Also by listening, not overlooking anyone and not settling for minimums—pushing them to maximums.
Questioner:	Again, what does that mean in practice? What do you do to get maximums?
Respondent:	Basically, you've got to have multiple backup assignments and several things ready for them to do. Those children who need more to do should get it; others might need to backtrack and relearn things; others are just less focused and need more help or options. Whatever level they're on you've got to keep them actively involved all the time. By emphasizing effort you can show you believe in them. If you don't stress effort they'll lapse into believing it's all ability—that you either have it or you don't. That's the last thing you want to have happen to children.

This star could offer a generalization and give specific examples of what holding this concept means in practice. This ability to go between theory and practice predicts that the individual responding in this way will continue to grow and benefit from subsequent staff development. This dialogue stands in sharp contrast to dialogues with quitter/failures who are 1) frequently unable or unwilling to generalize about what good teachers do, and 2) unable to connect any generalizations with what that idea would mean for the teacher's day-to-day practice. Without this ability to connect concepts of teaching with specific ways to implement these generalizations, teachers are unable to develop and improve. There can be no "inservice" other than having teachers replicate with children exactly what was taught to them. On the other hand, teachers who can connect ideas with practice can tick off innumerable ways in which they might adapt and apply an idea in their classrooms. Such teachers have an unlimited capacity for growth.

The process of connecting ideas—and ideals—to classroom behavior is especially valuable to teachers of children in poverty. The foregoing example, ("Good teachers have high expectations") is not merely a research-based generalization that can be used to increase student learning. It is also part of the star teacher's ideology. The need for teachers of diverse children in poverty to have both ideas and ideals makes this ability to connect concepts about teaching and learning to classroom practice an absolute requirement for effective teaching.

Star Teachers

I have avoided the use of the term learning theory in this discussion because there are no complete theories of learning that explain and predict school learning. There are numerous theoretic propositions, concepts and principles that have useful implications for teachers but no overall system for explaining and predicting the learning that occurs in classrooms. The one exception—behavior modification-- can be effective in preschool and primary grades. However, once children reach the stage of development in which pleasing peers is more important to them than pleasing teachers this approach loses its usefulness since the rewards students receive from peers are given for not doing schoolwork and demonstrating apathy.

The ability of quitter/failures to connect concepts of teaching and learning with classroom practice is minimal to nonexistent. Even when given an idea they are unable to suggest classroom practices that would implement it. Conversely, given a classroom practice they cannot explain the concept it illustrates. Consider the following group interview of six quitter/failures as they attempt to connect practice with an overall concept.

Questioner: Imagine you have observed me teach for half an hour for five days in a row. Each day I tell the whole class to turn to another page in their reading workbooks, page 58,59,60 etc. The children work quietly at their desks all completing the same assignment. Each works on his/her own. On the basis of these observations, what would you infer that I believe about good teaching? What do I believe about how children learn best?

Respondent #1:   I think you believe in trusting children.

Respondent #2:   I believe you are well organized and have planned well.

Respondent #3:   You probably believe in teamwork and will have the children share their answers later on.

Respondent #4:   Would you repeat the question? (This is done several times and the word 'infer' is replaced by the word 'think'. After several further requests for clarification the question is restated in first grade English as, 'If this is what I am doing, what do I think good teaching is?' Respondent #4 is still unable to make any response.)

Respondent #5:   I would think you're a good teacher.

Respondent #6:   I wouldn't generalize about you. That would be unfair.

Many readers will be surprised, even shocked, by the inability of college graduates who are certified teachers, ("fully qualified"), to deal with even this low level of discourse. I can only report that it happens regularly and that in the 45 years that I have asked these questions the responses of quitter/ failures have not changed.

This mid-range function of putting ideas into practice is an absolute necessity to the work of star teachers. Their ideals are stable over time, but the pool of ideas they use to implement their ideals is constantly expanding. They are constantly engaged in learning more about various subject matters, about how children learn together and alone and about the effects on culture and language from growing up in poverty. As stars pick up new concepts they are able to think up numerous ways of implementing them in their classrooms. But just as frequently, stars think in the reverse order. They are attracted by materials, equipment or an activity that will interest children— and they try it out. They are engaged in a continuous process of adopting and adapting new and better ideas. They remain completely and sensitively aware of why they are doing what they do, what they hope to accomplish and how doing it connects with everything else. In contrast to concretized non-thinkers, stars never lose sight of the ideology that undergirds every aspect of life in their classrooms. They reflect upon and seek to align their own and their students' behaviors with their ideology as a reminder of why they and the students are there.

K. Approach to At-Risk Students

When identifying the diverse groups of children in poverty educators constantly substitute terms they consider inoffensive for terms that have become offensive to particular groups.   These euphemisms inevitably become recognized for what they are —labels and code words. They might appear to be innocuous when they are originally adopted because they are new terms without a clear history. As these labels become familiar, however, it soon becomes clear in the public mind and among professional educators that the same groups are being identified: children with low achievement scores; children who are frequently absent; children whose families move frequently or are homeless; children from families in poverty; children who are frequently disciplined, suspended or expelled; children with handicapping conditions; children who don't use standard English; children whose parents are not visible in the school; children most likely to be victims of physical or chemical abuse; children who are more likely to become teenage parents; children who disappear, drop out or are sent to alternative schools; children of non-English speaking backgrounds; and adjudicated delinquents. Added to this list are the terms educators use to describe any children and youth they perceive as problems, i.e. students who learn less quickly, who are less willing to take constant direction and who teachers find less likeable. The term teachers have invented for students not doing well, but who cannot be labeled with some handicapping condition, is "gray area" children. Hanging over all these attributes is the unspoken assumption that all these terms are most likely to be describing students of color.

Those with handicapping physical, mental or emotional conditions that can be assessed by school psychologists are considered to be diagnosed rather than labeled. At present, there are over 6.5 million children and youth who have been formally identified as having some form of handicapping condition. This is approximately twelve percent of the children in public schools. By the year 2010, this number may well approach ten million or twenty percent of the students. Given the number of teachers who perceive of children with any problem, as children they shouldn't have to deal with, special education students may easily reach twenty-five percent of the total by 2012. In my own city we have eighteen percent of the children legally identified as abnormal and this number will soon reach twenty percent given the number who have been referred and are waiting to be tested. This means that one out of every five children in the urban district is supposedly abnormal in comparison to one out of one hundred in the surrounding suburbs. It is also important to note that there is a significantly disproportionate representation of children of color among those "diagnosed" as abnormal in some way. The State of Massachusetts has identified twenty-eight percent of its African American children as having some handicapping condition. These figures are truly staggering when one extrapolates them nationwide and considers that most of the youngsters labeled are concentrated in the 120 largest urban school districts.

THE MID-RANGE FUNCTIONS OF STARS WHICH CAN
BE ASSESSED IN INTERVIEWS

There are thirty-three million people living in poverty in America. In 2004, sixteen percent of all children (fourteen million) lived in poverty families. Approximately half of these live in rural areas and half in the major urban areas. The latter are the children in poverty from diverse cultural backgrounds who attend school in the 120 largest urban school districts.

The situation is quite clear. The number of children and youth who are perceived to be failing in school or doing significantly less well than they should be is high and growing...especially in urban school districts. If we add those labeled as abnormal in some way to those in poverty, (recognizing that these numbers are growing at a substantial rate), it would be accurate to define those labeled "at risk" as comprising the overwhelming majority of the school population in the 120 largest urban school districts. These include students teachers call "gray area" children who fall between the cracks of the system because they are not officially labeled as handicapped and do not receive any special services. Teachers claim to spend most of their time trying to bring gray area youngsters up to grade level, or disciplining them, or both. There are gray area children in every class. In urban schools it is typical for more than half of the class to be functioning below grade level. When we add gray area students to the previous two groups (the handicapped and those in poverty) we have now accounted for approximately half of the children and youth in American schools and approximately three quarters of those in urban schools. What this means in reality is that in our major urban districts teachers perceive their students as having problems that exceed their ability to compensate for them. How is it possible for schools and teachers to define a substantial majority of their clients as people they are unable to adequately teach?

The answer to this critical question provides the context for understanding the current situation related to "at risk" children and youth. In former times the children of the urban masses could skip high school entirely and still earn a decent living—even send their children to college. Because there were good jobs, even the undereducated could achieve upward mobility for themselves and their families. Today, the production and manufacturing jobs are abroad, not in the United States. This means that in spite of the fact that most students now complete high school and almost half attend some form of post secondary institution, graduates can no longer be assured that if they work hard they will be more successful than their parents. The families who understand this competition for a shrinking number of better jobs focus on pushing their children into getting into the more prestigious colleges and universities. As a result, the public has come to regard education as a personal good rather than a common good. The implication of this shift is that most people no longer see value in supporting schools for "other" people's children and see schooling as a personal commodity that benefits only the individual not society. Eighty percent of American families have no children in public K-12 schools. They respond to efforts aimed at equalizing educational opportunity with, "if you want more or better schooling you pay for it." Those with children in the top half believe they have earned the right to enter the better colleges and universities and pursue prestigious careers. Others—the bottom half—are provided schooling whose goal is "get a job and stay out of jail". These children are prepared with minimal basic skills for the low level jobs that do not lead to upward mobility or enriching careers. In effect, our society accepts, supports and maintains an educational process that inevitably produces winners from the same economic classes and culture groups who are currently the winners. If genuine equal opportunity were provided then those who benefit from the current system would be traumatized. Diverse children in poverty would have decent schools and would be able to compete successfully for the elite universities. As a result, the high status jobs with economic and political power would be equally distributed between diverse children from poverty backgrounds and those from middle class and professional backgrounds. Similarly, the menial jobs in our society—including military service—would be equally distributed among all socio-economic classes. The notion that those who benefit from the current dysfunctional system value equal educational opportunity enough to threaten the life chances of their own children is a fantasy. For diverse students in poverty the agreed-upon goal of the larger society is to educate them to be happy, compliant losers rather than antisocial ones.

Against this background—which might be described as the rhetoric of equal opportunity versus the reality of an inferior education for diverse children in poverty—we now return to the question: How is it possible for schools and teachers to define a majority of their clients as people who shouldn't be there, or individuals they are unable to teach, or as students not ready for their particular grade level or subject matter?

THE MID-RANGE FUNCTIONS OF STARS WHICH CAN
BE ASSESSED IN INTERVIEWS

In New York City, in 1800, children newly arrived from London slums were taught in classes of 1,000 by one schoolmaster and a pyramid of monitors, arranged by age, who repeated his lessons verbatim to all the others. In the two centuries since then, urban public schools have still not provided children in poverty with equal educational opportunity. The theories and research we have used to create the fields of child and adolescent development were developed to explain the behavior of white, middle class Christian, Americans. Everyone outside of this experience is regarded as an exception, whether from another class, race, religion, language group, country or nontraditional family. The concept of average or typical is used synonymously with normal. Normal is then made synonymous with healthy and desirable. Future teachers are taught that these "normal" characteristics are universal in their application to children and youth from all groups when in fact they are parochial, middle-class American attributes. As a result of learning about children and youth from this cultural knothole, a majority of the children in the world are defined as different, special or abnormal in some way. Future teachers, under the burden of this "knowledge" in their teacher education programs are not merely unprepared for a diverse America but destined to fail in it. Imagine the impact of teacher education programs in which young, late-adolescent, white females (ages 18-22) learn the supposedly universal characteristics of normal, healthy children and youth and are then placed in diverse urban classrooms! Is it any wonder that a majority of our urban children and youth are perceived as abnormal by their teachers? Such irrelevant teacher education can only be perpetrated by education faculty who have themselves not taught diverse children in urban poverty and who are not held accountable for turning out graduates who are quitter/failures. And this is precisely the case. Less than five percent of teacher educators have taught in urban schools for three years or more. Faculty in education departments still raise questions such as, "Kids are kids! Learning is learning. Good teaching is good teaching! So what's different about teaching in urban schools?" To admit that their theories and concepts of "normal" are limited by culture, class, language, race and ethnicity would be to admit that the teacher preparation they offer is not universal. To admit that they have not been teaching universal concepts would raise questions about their academic expertise, and thus, their right to hold positions as faculty members. Further, the practice of state departments of education awarding teaching licenses that proclaim the bearers "fully qualified" to teach all children in all settings would be called into question. Clearly, many constituent groups have a vested interest (their positions, status, authority, salaries and retirements) in maintaining the fiction that the concepts of child and adolescent development taught to teachers in university based teacher education programs are universal.

Even greater than the problem of not having a valid knowledge base for knowing what is normal is that there is nothing in traditional teacher education programs to counteract the various forms of prejudice and racism with which preservice students in America begin their teaching preparation studies and careers. Racism, sexism, bias against non-English speakers, and most of all, misconceptions about why people are poor, are as common among future teachers as in the population at large. Preservice students' typical explanations of poverty include the full range of stereotypes: the poor are stupid, lazy, without initiative, and lacking in moral responsibility for themselves and their families. Non-existent universal principles of child development as well as prejudices and misconceptions about why there are poor people in the United States comprises the "knowledge base" which launches certified graduates into their careers as teachers of diverse children in urban poverty in failing school districts. Compounding these handicaps, the neophyte begins his/her career consumed with fear regarding discipline. The most pressing, all-consuming question asked by beginning teachers is, "Will I be able to control the class?" This is a natural and understandable reaction to children and youth they fear and do not understand or respect. This fear and prejudice has been carefully taught by defining most of the children and youth as not "normal" (i.e. handicapped, disadvantaged, at-risk, gray area) in their ability to learn, speak and behave. The natural consequence of holding this view of the clients is an obsession with controlling them. Given this view of the teacher's role, the fearful neophyte grasps at authoritarian methods of instruction as necessary for controlling the class. Beginning with this need to dominate rather than relate to their students, the newly certified graduates of traditional teacher education programs (i.e. the "fully qualified") have been systematically and carefully prepared to be quitter/failures in schools serving diverse children and youth in urban poverty. The teacher churn, i.e. the turnover of new teachers in the 120 major urban areas, has been a well documented phenomenon over more than half a century. It is a result of the ignorant training the fearful to do the irrelevant.

Dysfunctional teacher education is a major part of the explanation for why a majority of children and youth in urban districts are defined as exceptional or special in some way. The school districts encourage this because they receive substantially greater federal and state aid for supporting the labeling process. Any label attached to any group of children will be welcomed by the district if there can be increased funding for having such children. In my city, the school district receives approximately $200 million per year for labeling more and more children as handicapped. Failing schools are faced with a forced choice. Either the professional staff lacks the know-how to teach the children, or there are things wrong with the children that prevent the professional staff from being effective. It is infinitely easier and certainly more profitable to categorize the children as special or handicapped than to transform failing school districts into effective ones. To protect against law suits it is also necessary to focus on the inadequacies and failures of the clients rather than the ineffective services provided by dysfunctional school bureaucracies.

Blaming the victim is actively pursued by teachers, school districts, teacher preparing institutions, teacher credentialing agencies and by state and federal grant givers. Indeed, blaming the victim is an occupational disease of educators. In former times we used terms such as culturally deprived, disadvantaged, academically underdeveloped, difficult to serve, hard to reach, alienated, disaffected and a host of others. All of these terms, including the present "at risk", are labels used for the same purpose: to attribute the causes of low achievement and school failure to the children and their families and not to schools and teachers. These labels make it appear that that the labeler is merely being diagnostic not prejudicial. But there is no way to provide a high quality or even equal education to children who are perceived and labeled as basically inadequate or abnormal.

The reason the labeling process for diverse children in poverty never ends is that there are only one of two alternatives. The teachers having problems must perceive inadequacies in the children, or inadequacies in themselves and their methods. Either the child must change or the teacher must. If neither can change someone is at fault. If there is widespread failure, as in urban schools, then blame is readily placed on the victims. To do otherwise would mean that the teachers do not know enough, do not use the best methods, or do not have the ability to relate to the children. It is interesting that when there is success, the teachers do not "blame" the students for learning effectively but are most willing to accept complete responsibility and full accountability for their students' learning.

When asked to explain the large number of students at-risk of failing or dropping out, quitter/failure teachers go through the same litany of causes as those without teacher training: dysfunctional families, drugs, violence, gangs, lack of health care, poor housing, unemployment, crime, lack of belief in education, no role models and physical defects. If specifically asked: "How do you explain the majority of students in urban schools being behind in basic skills?" they make no attribution whatever to inadequacies in schooling. They do not criticize schools or teachers. They see only failings in the victim, his family and community. To solve these problems they propose ways in which all the other agencies of society outside of schools might help families and children improve their lives and better prepare children to benefit from the opportunities offered in their schools. Not only do they not see schools and curricula as needing to become more responsive, they do not consider that they as teachers must change what they do. Indeed, quitter/failures justify their perceptions with comments such as, "What am I suppose to do about hunger or child abuse? Or, "I'm a teacher not a nurse or a social worker!" Polls of the general public indicate quite clearly that most Americans agree with these perceptions that the victims themselves are primarily to blame for the failure of urban schools.

The ideology of star teachers is completely different. They know all of the same explanations of what is wrong with many of the families and communities in which the children live. Stars will mention all of the same causes of children and youth being at-risk as others, but they do not stop there. They also cite the variety of ways in which school curricula and teaching methods contribute to causing so many children to be labeled at risk. Their ideology focuses on the school. They mention irrelevant curriculum, boring teachers and authoritarian methods as exacerbating the problem. Essentially stars say, "Look, I exert the most control over what and how I teach. I should be able to find ways of involving my students in learning no matter what their out-of-school lives are like. That's my job and that's what I work at. I find activities and projects that turn them on to learning." This does not mean that stars are insensitive to the problems and impact of poverty. They focus on their roles as teachers and accept responsibility for students' learning.

How the teacher explains and thinks about at-risk students is the most powerful predictor of his/her success in teaching diverse children in poverty. Quitter/failures justify their lack of effectiveness by becoming experts in the children's inadequacies. They seem to want to know as much as possible about their children for the specific purpose of proving that teaching these children is impossible. Stars, on the other hand, learn as much as possible about their children for entirely different motives. They seek to learn more about the children's backgrounds because they genuinely care about them. They seek information that might help them with a referral to a health or human service agency that might get the child and his family more services. At other times, they might do the extra work of reporting cases of abuse or neglect. The most important reason stars want to learn more about their students' out-of-school lives is that they want to make learning more meaningful and relevant. Information about their students enables stars to make specific connections between what is being taught in class and something that will clinch its meaning for a particular student. Stars also know that by listening to what their children tell them about their lives, they are deepening the bonds of mutual respect between themselves and their students. In sum, quitter/failures do not necessarily know less than stars about the children they teach. The critical difference is whether teachers use this information to "prove" the child cannot be taught or doesn't belong in their classroom, versus whether they use information about students to make school curriculum more meaningful to them.

Of all the mid-range functions that discriminate between stars and quitter/failures, this dimension is the most powerful predictor of teacher effectiveness and staying power. There is no question that those predisposed to blame the victim have one option: they will fail as teachers of children in poverty. Those whose ideologies lead them to seek more effective teaching strategies, regardless of youngsters' backgrounds, have a good chance of becoming effective teachers of diverse children in poverty.

What this mid-range function means for those who hire teachers is that it predicts whether the teachers they hire will accept personal accountability for their students' learning. Teachers who feel the students are to blame for low achievement are in effect telling the school district in advance that when the children do not reach acceptable levels of learning that they will respond with "What do you want from me?" School districts should only hire teachers who will accept being held accountable and who, when faced with low achievement, will respond, "There's got to be a better way; it's up to me to find it and I know I can do it!"

L. Professional versus Personal Orientation

Do stars believe they must love their children in order to teach them? Do stars believe the children must love their teachers in order to learn from them? The answer to both questions is a resounding "no". Stars use words like respect, caring and trust. In many cases stars do come to love their children, but they know that love is not a method of teaching or the basis of the teacher-student relationship. Many quitter/failures are quickly disillusioned when the students they claim to love do not follow their directions or misbehave. Professional teachers know how to relate to children in a supportive professional manner, even when they do despicable things. Stars are keenly aware of and honest about the fact that many of the children and youth they teach are not lovable.

As with all the other mid-range functions of star teachers this one is a combination of actual teacher behaviors supported by an undergirding ideology. Whether the teacher takes a personal orientation to teaching (love) or a professional one (respect) goes to the very core of the individual's motivation for becoming a teacher. What motivates an individual to become a teacher? Why does an individual remain in teaching? What does the teacher see as the basis of the teacher-student relationship? How does a teacher manage a classroom and a system of discipline? What personal needs (outside of monetary and health coverage) is a teacher seeking to satisfy by becoming a teacher?

The ideology of star teachers leads them to answer these questions in terms of what's best for the students, not in terms of satisfying their own emotional needs. Stars establish very close and personal relationships with the children they teach. These relationships have many aspects of a love relationship. But stars recognize the dangers of such relationships and do not fall into the trap of needing children's love for their own emotional support. They do not feed on children. They understand that the basic goal of the teacher is to connect children with meaningful subject matter in ways that will make them lifelong learners. Their primary goal is to lead their students to learn useful, valuable content. Stars do not believe they can accomplish this by simply loving children or expecting the children to love them.

The scenario of quitter/failures is quite different. They expect to love the children who will do nice things because they love their teacher and then they, in turn, can love the children for being so nice. When they realize that all the children are not "nice" they discover they do not love them. And when children respond to their directions with less than lovable behaviors they panic. They realize their pet cliché, "I want to be a teacher because I love children", is neither a strategy of teaching nor a method of controlling students' behavior.

Many parents control their children by inspiring guilt. They use their hurt feelings and disappointment to control their children's behavior. "If you really love me you would do this and not that." Or, "If you really love me you will do this even though you find it difficult or even upsetting. Do it for me!" This ability to generate guilt by using love appears to work for some parents, if by "work" we mean that they can control some of their children's behaviors. Actually, it more frequently does not "work" because children do not develop an intrinsic desire to engage in the behaviors parents prefer and once they are not directly supervised they will frequently stop the behavior or do the opposite. Psychologists and counselors do a land office business with adults whose parents tried to control them with guilt when they were children.

The parental basis for relating to their children is to provide unconditional love. The teachers' basis for relating to children is professional: i.e. to teach all their students as much as possible regardless of how they feel about them. Teachers are legally not en loco parentis (i.e. in place of parents) and should not seek to emulate their role. It is quite easy for many teachers, particularly those who teach young children, to take on the parental role. This appears to be a workable relationship for many who actually define themselves as "huggers" and in other ways which signal their love. There are critical differences between stars and quitter/failures in this regard. Stars are aware of the danger of using children to fill emotional lacks in their own lives. They are not wounded healers seeking to compensate for what is missing in their own lives by feeding emotionally on children. They have their own families, adult relationships and significant others who provide emotional support outside of the classroom. They thoroughly respect and care deeply about their children, but their relationship is a professional one that also separates them from the children. And their caring has the clear goal of fostering learning. Stars also demonstrate respect for the children by not exploiting the close relationships they build with them. In return, the children come to see stars as people they care about and respect. The teachers are seen as models and the children seek to try out their behaviors: e.g. reading for enjoyment, writing to express oneself, conducting experiments, building models, speaking other languages, using computers for research, asking and answering endless questions. By building trusting, supportive, respectful, professional relationships with children stars become the models children seek to emulate.

Stars are sensitive and aware of the fact that the process of building trusting relationships takes time and that the children they begin with in September may have had years of conditioning at only working for extrinsic rewards. Even stars use extrinsic rewards—at the beginning. It is very likely that in the beginning children will be encouraged to try out a subject or an activity simply to please the teacher or for a sticker or food. But as the teacher builds a relationship of respect and trust with the children the modeling effect begins to take effect. "If Mrs. Smith seems to enjoy it so much and cares so much that I give it a try, maybe I will." In relationships where the children have negative feelings toward their teacher the reverse is likely to occur. Stars are sensitive to how this dynamic works. The child's initial impetus for engaging in an activity may be to model teacher behavior, but over time, this is transformed into an intrinsically rewarding involvement with the particular subject. This means that the teacher provides the children with choices, involves them in planning their activities, and gives them some real decision-making power over how they will pursue their learning activities. Stars may start out using some extrinsic rewards because that is what the children have been taught to believe is appropriate behavior. But after the teacher demonstrates respect and caring, the motivation shifts to modeling teacher behavior. And as the teacher-student relationship deepens further and the students have more experiences with interesting learning activities, star teachers move the students to see that the greatest rewards come from the feelings they derive from being successful at their work and the intrinsic joy of learning new and interesting things.

Stars are also sensitive to the reality that there will be children, perhaps several in each class, who are not prime candidates for "lovable child of the year." Their approach to these children is equally caring and respectful. Stars know full well that if they made "love" the prerequisite for teaching and learning they would have to write off several children in every class.

Stars are also sensitive to the reality that they must be sensitive to their students' life conditions. When cases of abuse, neglect and health issues surface they become directly involved by making referrals and seeking the assistance of others in the school. At the same time stars are very careful about not intruding into the life space of their students. They do not seek information for its own sake; neither do they offer unsolicited advice regarding matters not directly related to learning in the classroom.

This love issue is especially important in understanding effective classroom management and discipline. Stars set up rules to govern behavior in the classroom, in school and on trips that are few in number but which have logical consequences for themselves and the children. The reasons for these rules are discussed and reviewed on a regular basis so that everyone sees their sense and usefulness. It cannot be stated strongly enough that this simple process of setting up and following the classroom rules "works" because the teacher has established a relationship of trust and respect with the children. A teacher without this relationship can set up the very same rules and follow the very same procedures and they will not "work". This is why beginning teachers and quitter/failure teachers are so fearful (correctly so) of classroom management and discipline. The process of setting up a few classroom rules and following them is easy for beginning teachers to set out and follow, but has no value apart from who the teacher is. It is only in the hands of a teacher who has built a relationship with the children that the process "works". Quitter/failures and others frequently do not understand this dynamic and conclude that in matters of discipline some teachers simply "have it and some don't". What they do not understand is that the stars' ideology enables them to effectively relate to children because they communicate feelings of respect. Stars never seek to manipulate children with guilt. ("How could you do this to me when I trusted you?") Stars expect and plan for times when even their most cooperative students will engage in negative behaviors. Stars' reaction is not to demonstrate a sense of being betrayed but to patiently pursue the logical consequences of whatever has occurred. Stars' ability to support and nurture children who have engaged in wrongful, even despicable acts, derives from the fact that they truly care about the children but have not fallen into the trap of having a love relationship with them. As professionals they never forget that these are children in the throes of growing up, not perpetrators in need of greater punishments. Stars' caring is not predicated on children always doing the right thing. On the contrary, it assumes they frequently will not. Their professional caring demonstrates to the students that they are worthy of respect even at the worst and lowest moments of their offensive behavior. What stars show children is not "You have hurt me and let me down." But rather that things have occurred which are truly regrettable and unwise but "We are in this together and will have to work it out together." This is just one more indication that stars have more emotional stamina than other teachers. They may have invested countless hours in school and after school with youngsters only to see them drop out, use drugs, get pregnant, become involved in crime and even be killed. Nevertheless they continue to invest themselves in their students. I recently spoke with two middle school teachers who had children in their classrooms murdered. They were consumed with grief and could not discuss the children without weeping. Yet they were back at school the very next day building supportive relationships with their students. By not using instances of personal tragedy to distance themselves from their children, stars demonstrate great emotional stamina. It would be easy for veteran stars to eventually conclude, "What's the use! You give all your time and energy and they let you down." Instead they take the professional approach. "So long as there are children to be taught who need my services and whose lives will be turned around by learning, I will be there." Quitter/failure teachers frequently adopt "love" as a teaching strategy because they assume that they can use love to control. After all, "you wouldn't do something nasty to someone who loves you." When they learn that children "I have done absolutely everything for" still misbehave they have lost the basic strategy they depended on for control. This assumption that teaching must be based on love is most common among teachers of young children. They give the most directions, provide the most external rewards for following directions and regard compliance as "cooperation". It is not accidental that teachers who believe love is the basis of their relationship with children are also the most likely to recommend that those who are not lovable need to be tested for some category of special education. Following is a typical dialogue with a teacher who believes in love as the basis of the teacher-student relationship.

Questioner:	Is it necessary for you to love all the children in order to teach them?
Respondent:	Yes. I love all children.
Questioner:	You've never met a child you didn't love?
Respondent:	Not yet.
Questioner:	Can you imagine having a child in class that is not necessarily lovable?
Respondent:	I may not like what he does, but I still love him.
Questioner:	If a student slashed your tires you would still love him?
Respondent:	None of my children would do that, but yes I would still love him.
Questioner:	Can you imagine a child who doesn't necessarily love you?
Respondent:	Yes, at first.
Questioner:	Would you still be able to teach such a child?
Respondent:	Yes.
Questioner:	Why is it necessary for you to love each child but not necessary for each child to love you?
Respondent:	Over time, as that child comes to appreciate all that I am doing for him, he will learn to love me.
Questioner:	I want to make certain that I understand what you are saying. You believe that loving the student is a prerequisite to teaching him anything.
Respondent:	Yes. It's the basis for teaching.
Questioner:	Do you love everyone now in the Cook County Jail?
Respondent:	(Pause) I'm not sure. Probably not.
Questioner:	Is it possible that you could teach something to some of the inmates?

STAR TEACHERS

Respondent: (Pause) Perhaps. I'm not sure. I wouldn't want to try.

Questioner: In any event we can be clear. Your view is that love is the basis for teachers being able to teach and children being able to learn.

Respondent: Right.

This interview is of a teacher who will undoubtedly fail as a teacher of diverse children in poverty. The expectation that mutual love is the basis of the teacher-student relationship will be shattered as soon as the teacher sees that she doesn't love "these" children and the students feel no obligation to pretend they love her. I recall visiting a middle school teacher who sat quietly at her desk weeping while the class was in chaos. This teacher confided to me, "I don't know why they behave this way. I take them places every weekend. I bring them home evenings. I really do love these kids." At the end of the period as the children filed out, a student put her arms around the still weeping teacher and said encouragingly, "Don't take it personal Ms. B. that's the way kids are." I found it interesting that while the teacher didn't know the basis of a professional relationship, this thirteen year old student did. What the student was really telling Ms. B. was "Relate to us on a professional level and don't take what we do as a personal affront."

The situation in our urban schools today is that teachers must be able to demonstrate respect and caring without ever touching a student. Every urban system in the country has pending court cases of teachers who touched a child for some good and appropriate reason. No matter how these cases get decided the advice to teachers is always the same, "In your role as a professional teacher there is no justification for you to touch a student." We must get away from the stereotype of the maternal mother substitute who claims to be a "hugger" and recognize the reality of teaching in a complex, diverse society. Would we want the teacher of high school math hugging his students for getting right answers? How are college students able to learn from faculty they do not love and professors able to teach students without loving them? Those who take the untenable position that love is necessary for learning, but only for young children, must tell us at what age it stops being a necessary condition of learning.

The mid-range function described here reflects star teachers' ideology for relating to students so that students learn more and develop a love of learning …not of them. Stars relate closely and positively to students, but do not intrude on their life space and do not use their relationships with children to meet their own unmet emotional needs. Stars seek to create students who will be independent and not need them. Quitter/failures seek the reverse; students who will be entirely dependent on them for approval. Stars do not regard love as a strategy of classroom discipline. Quitter/failures do. It is interesting that teaching is the only profession that suffers from this delusion. Accountants, dentists, social workers, nurses, psychiatrists and all other professionals would find this discussion entirely unnecessary, even absurd. It is only in teaching that loving the client is even discussed. The greatest teachers are those whose students believe their accomplishments represent things they learned on their own.

M. Burnout: The Care and Feeding of the Bureaucracy

The 120 urban school districts are all failing to some degree. Whether we use achievement data, attendance or graduation rates, they are all failing to provide seven million diverse students in poverty with reasonable, let alone equal, educational opportunities.

Stars are extremely sensitive to the fact that they work in debilitating bureaucracies. They are well aware of the fact that in the large urban school districts the teachers are treated like functionaries not professionals. Many of these districts now hire teachers by computerized interviews and paperwork. It is possible to be hired as a teacher in many of the major urban districts without ever having to speak to a human being. There is no other job I have ever been able to identify, from working in a car wash to cleaning toilets, where an individual can be hired without ever having to speak face-to-face with another human being. The directors of the human service departments of these school districts actually boast of how they have increased their efficiency at processing large numbers of teacher applicants by using computerized systems for conducting interviews and completing applications. They never stop to consider that if their systems for hiring new teachers were effective they would not need to hire so many new teachers again every year. These computerized interviews and impersonal application procedures consistently identify and select quitter/failures. The human resource staffs keep themselves extremely busy hiring new failure/quitters every year.

There are countless other examples of how the dysfunctional bureaucracies depersonalize the conditions of work. For example, it used to be that when teachers were ill and absent from school at least the school secretary knew about it because she had to call a substitute. Now, the teacher calls in to an automated system which calls substitutes. No one in the school office may even know that a teacher is out unless someone specifically tries to find her for some reason.

To the uninitiated, the school bureaucracy is simply comprised of administrators and regulations making it more difficult for good things to happen. To able, experienced teachers in urban systems, however, the school bureaucracy is recognized for what it is: an institutionalized set of privileged positions generating regulations which systematically prevent effective teaching and learning from taking place. The primary goal of the bureaucracy is to protect, enhance and enlarge itself.

It is not uncommon for a typical classroom to be interrupted over 125 times per week. There are students coming and going, messengers, the intercom, visitors, emergencies, office requests and special teachers pulling out students. The stated purpose of the school is that "learning is the highest priority", but the real priorities of schools are clearly demonstrated in the transient nature of life in classrooms which resemble bus terminals more than a places of learning.

Experienced teachers have become so inured to this constant stream of interruptions that they no longer resent or even notice it. In my programs we advise beginning teachers to put a sign on their doors that reads, "Testing. Do Not Enter" if they want to be certain they will not be interrupted.

But these are only a few of countless examples of how urban school districts have become self-serving bureaucracies organized for the convenience of everyone who works in them—except teachers and students. In 1990, there was a 1:1 ratio of classroom teachers to other adults employed in the urban systems. (This ratio does not take bus drivers into account.) Ostensibly all these employees are vitally needed to help in the teaching learning process or in supportive services. What this means is that there as many aides, paraprofessionals, assistant principals, principals, guidance counselors, school psychologists, social workers, nurses, Title I. teachers, reading resource teachers, math consultants, safety personnel and central office staff, as there are classroom teachers carrying a full teaching load working directly with children. Currently this ratio of teachers to others employed in the school districts is up to 2:1 in many urban systems and is approaching 3:1 in some. In my own city there are approximately 6,200 classroom teachers and the district admits to 12,500 employees (a 2:1 ratio), but 17, 000 individuals draw some sort of monthly payment from the district. This compares with schools in small town America, where failing districts are rare and in which teachers comprise 70 percent or more of the district's employees. Yet when urban districts are forced to make budget cuts they cut teachers first (letting class sizes rise) and protect the jobs of those who do not work directly with students. Urban districts try to cover up this practice of firing teachers first by counting all the system's certified employees, whether or not they directly teach children and then dividing this number into the total number of students enrolled. This enables them to claim that there is an 18:1 (or even lower ratio) of "certificated staff" to students. What they don't report is that most of these certificated personnel do not work directly with children as the official classroom teachers of record.

It is quite clear who benefits from failing urban school districts. The most powerful operating value in the urban school district is: The further you work from children the higher your status and salary. The more direct contact you have with children the lower your status and salary. This phenomenon of rampant, self-serving school bureaucracy is a reflection of big city political activity that is as American as apple pie. The primary goal is for the bureaucracy to feed itself and grow—always at the expense of the children it ostensibly serves. Politicians and others in depressed urban areas actually take credit for providing jobs to their constituents in these bloated bureaucracies. In every one of the 120 major cities in America the largest local employer is the school district. The local school districts are the engines driving the economies of the American city.

STAR TEACHERS

The bureaucratic conditions fostering the miseducation of children in urban poverty apply to many smaller urban school systems as well as to the 120 largest ones. In one depressed urban area of Indiana where I conducted a research project for three years, there were 480 teachers who worked with children and youth. This relatively small staff was "helped" by an equal number of administrators and other employees. Five of the seven city councilmen were on the school budget in some capacity. The school district listed four individuals with the title "Athletic Director". One individual who was related to a school board member was paid $45,000 per year to make the daily announcements over the intercom each morning at one of the high schools…and that was the total extent of his duties. Yet, the school district is officially designated by the state as "bankrupt". The children have outdated or no texts. In most classrooms the teacher has the only text. Book publishers, indeed no suppliers of any educational materials or equipment, will deal with this district. It has unpaid bills dating back twenty-five years. The way the school bureaucracy survives is by spreading its funds among the very individuals who have the power to change the system but who choose not to in favor of benefiting themselves at the expense of the district. Such corruption is not atypical in our urban districts. What differs is the extent of the corruption and the strategies used by the beneficiaries.

The characteristics of dysfunctional urban school bureaucracies are as follows:

1. Superintendents come and go, but at great expense to the districts that must buy out their contracts. I know of many superintendents who have been bought out to leave their positions and currently serve as superintendents in new ones. Failure superintendents who keep moving can collect two paychecks per month representing annual salaries that are eight times or more than the salaries of great teachers who remain teaching in these dysfunctional districts.

2. These systems are highly centralized. Their rhetoric is about decentralization, but what they decentralize to the schools is accountability for student achievement. What they keep for themselves in the central office is control of the budget and all the decision-making authority that ensures the system will continue to benefit the central office administrators.

3. The orientation of the chain of command is only downward. Ideas and policies originate with higher levels. Lower levels are to comply and implement. The system, thus, precludes the creativity and energy that characterizes successful organizations.

4. The downward flow of directives generates an upward flow of misinformation and disinformation from anxious subordinates. As a result, the widespread use of false achievement data and false drop out data from schools to central office is quite common in the urban districts.

5. Central offices must dissemble to stay in control. No major urban school district in America honestly reports the number of its employees, or the actual costs of particular programs. The use of complex accounting programs systematically co-mingle federal, state, local and private funds so that the exact cost of any program, or office, or service can never be fully or accurately known.

6. The organization of the bureaucracy inevitably proliferates numerous isolated units which are supposed to work cooperatively. The system of rewards, however, i.e. jobs, salary, benefits, promotions security, is all dispensed to individuals in the separate units, thus, discouraging cooperation or articulation.

7. Particular administrative units protect themselves from budget cuts by constantly seeking to expand themselves. There is an inevitable and constant tug of war among organizational units to compete for and gain higher budgets, none of which are directly relevant to the work of teachers and the learning of children.

8. There is an irresistible pressure created to support and protect the central office bureaucracy. This motivation to protect the system—and the particular organizational units within the system—occurs at the expense of the stated goals of improving the learning of students. Every new superintendent vows to change this but merely ends up reorganizing the same cast of thousands into new self-serving units. Urban superintendents inevitably leave bigger central offices after them

than they inherited; the more vociferous their promises to cut, the bigger the central office they are likely to leave for the next superintendent.

9. Selective rule following and the selective enforcement of rules are used to prevent or derail any serious change effort. Bureaucratic functionaries are ingenious and flexible at circumventing rules, policies and union contracts in order to gain some personal advantage. They then rigidly use these very same rules to block any change efforts which threaten the benefits they derive from maintaining the current system.

10. Many central office personnel are originally drawn from the schools, but as time passes they lose any notion of what is currently going on in them. As they become more isolated from the schools their activities and the policies they promote become increasingly remote, irrelevant and obstacles to teaching and learning.

11. Decisions are all made in committees so that there is no way to hold anyone accountable for the failure of any policy, program, grant, or other initiative.

12. Second and third level functionaries play a cloying and subservient role to top level superintendents, superintendent appointees and board members. At the same time these lower level personnel know they must survive the top levels people who come and go. As a result, these lower level functionaries are constantly engaged in covering themselves and their actions so that they can disassociate themselves from the present administration and its policies at some future time. In effect, the very people whom the superintendents and school boards expect to implement their policies with enthusiasm and vigor are actively involved in planning how they will protect themselves from the failure of these initiatives. The bureaucrat's primary function is to survive the present administration, not to make it work.

Legislators and others typically attempt to correct these systems by cutting their budgets. Such cutting doesn't work for a simple reason. The bureaucrats absorb budget cuts by cutting teachers and others, not central office functionaries such as themselves. For the last half century private foundations, state legislatures, the business community and local citizen's groups have attempted to fight the growth of urban school bureaucracy by supporting a variety of initiatives: decentralization, community control, site-based management, neighborhood school boards and more recently, parent vouchers and charter schools. In spite of countless well-financed change efforts, school bureaucracies not only survive, but continue to expand. Class size and teacher loads continue to grow—except in high schools. This is because substantial numbers of middle schoolers have quit or not passed the high stakes tests needed to enter high school. Other high school students are ghosts carried on the attendance registers for state support, but never attend. The bureaucracies of the urban school districts have proven so impenetrable to change that every major private foundation has stopped making grants to them except for very narrowly defined purposes that they can monitor themselves. These are usually small grants made directly to teachers, or student scholarships which completely circumvent the bureaucracy.

Star teachers are well aware of these conditions. While they are sensitive to and conscious of how they and their children are being exploited by school bureaucracies, they spend little or no time tilting against these windmills. They are as aware of this dysfunctionality as critics and analysts, but their commitment to their children's learning motivates them to adjust, cope and remain in these bureaucracies. Quitter/failures on the other hand, are crushed because they do not draw the same energy from interacting with children and youth. Also, they are less sensitive to the pressures that come from the system itself and take no actions to mitigate its negative impact.

Burnout is an occupational disease faced by all urban teachers. The following analysis details the differences in ideology and behaviors between stars and others as they seek to resolve or prevent the negative organizational pressures on teachers. These are pressures to do less, try less, work in isolation, blame the victim and pretend that all the people who work in urban schools hold the educational welfare of children rather than their own jobs, benefits and convenience as their highest goal.

Stars recognize that even good teachers burn out and that the organizational press of a dysfunctional bureaucracy is an inevitable source of constant stress. Stars protect themselves in several ways: by learning which rules and policies must be obeyed and which can be ignored; by learning which paperwork and clerical demands must be met and which can be delayed or put off indefinitely; and by learning what to read and not read in their mailboxes. This quality— the care and feeding of the bureaucracy—is a critical part of the stars' craft. Stars do not set out to anger or threaten administrators and system functionaries. At the same time, they want to spend as little time as possible on paper work and out-of-class functions that does not directly involve them with their students. They do not want the time and energy they need to be effective with their students drawn off and expended on maintaining the organization. They believe that since there are more administrators and staff than there are teachers that these individuals should be helping them. In order to protect themselves and their children, stars become experts at how the school bureaucracy works, not because they seek to change it, but because they seek to do the absolute least that is necessary to feed it and in return, be left alone. I recall one star teacher with several cartons of papers in her closet. I asked what they were and she slyly winked and replied that they were notices from the school office. She had saved them all over the last three years and said that she would read them when she retired four years hence.

This function of protecting themselves from self-serving bureaucracies is a critical mid-range function. Stars reach a comfort level early in their careers and seek to maintain it. As they gain experience they hone their skill for deciding which notices to read and which to discard, which meetings to attend and which to skip, when to volunteer and when to duck, which duties to perform and which to have a child or aide do, when to use a telephone and when to perform a task in person. With these highly developed skills stars are able to garner and guard almost all their time and energy for teaching children. Without these skills and lacking the sensitivity that they even need such skills, quitter/failures are worn down by the system and have less and less time and energy for their teaching. This function is strange in the sense that, if it is done well, few will recognize the need for it or its great importance. If ignored or not done well, the bureaucracy becomes a formidable, daily obstacle to the work of the teacher. In analyzing endless lists of effective teacher behaviors and attributes I have never seen any traditional university based teacher education program which prepares candidates to perform this critical function. My hunch is that since college faculty have not worked in urban schools for any sustained period, if at all, they are knowledge-free of the need to perform this function. Yet, it is absolutely required. In my interviews of star teachers every single one has identified this function as vital to her/his success and survival and has been able to explain in detail how it is performed.

In addition to protecting themselves, stars have an even more important stake in the care and feeding of the bureaucracy. They seek to protect their children. They view themselves as lubricants between their children and the gears of the system. Just a few of the endless rules that directly affect the teachers and children refer to questions such as the following: When are field trips permissible and under what conditions? When and for what activities is insurance coverage needed? What material and equipment may and may not be brought into a classroom? Who is and who is not allowed in a classroom? What types of animals and plants may be kept? What written reports filed by what dates are the teachers responsible for? What kinds of homework are allowed and disallowed? When and under what conditions may a teacher speak with parents? What kinds of visual materials may be used and how is permission obtained? A teacher cannot walk the children around the block without a series of permissions. What constitutes decorating a room and what constitutes interference with the work of union painters, or breaks some rule in the fire code?

Stars also learn as much as possible about the informal structure of the school so that they do not miss out on learning how things really work. They know which secretary, which janitor, which safety aide and which other teachers will help them do what they want with the least paperwork, permissions or hassle. Stars are experts at using this informal structure to make the system work for them and their children. While quitter/failures are frustrated by running into brick walls and soon give up, the children in stars' classrooms are engaged in real learning activities—many of which are against school policy or, more likely, unknown to the formal bureaucracy.

A major feature of stars' teaching is to make learning as real and as relevant as possible for their children. This requires that their classrooms have more materials and equipment than others. It also means that they may have things not typically seen in classrooms, from living things to the greasy parts of a lawn mower. Stars also implement this reality by taking more field trips than others. They also spill over into other rooms, laboratories and spaces throughout the school. This practice of making learning real by using space, materials, equipment, direct experiences and resource people inevitably brings stars into conflict with the school bureaucracy. When stars add the practice of protecting their classes from interruptions, scheduling, clerical and other system demands, it soon becomes apparent that, in one way or another, they are in an almost constant posture of mitigating the negative impact of the school bureaucracy. Without the ability to perform this function—developed to a high level —stars would not be able to teach. Nowhere is the irrelevancy and failure of traditional forms of teacher education as clear as in its inability to prepare teachers to perform this function. Young, beginning teachers are sent to their demise by college and university faculty who are ignorant of or unable to deal with these dysfunctional school bureaucracies. Fifty percent of beginners are gone in five years, and in many districts in only three. This inability to survive in chaotic and intentionally self-serving school organizations is a primary cause.

A final note is in order. Stars do not function as isolates. They seek to set up networks of like-minded colleagues who serve as a support group. Because there may not be a sufficient number of teachers who agree with their practices they frequently set up a support group comprised of individuals who not all may be teachers. In many cases stars use several support groups because certain individuals may agree with just one aspect of their teaching, e.g. the use of field trips, or computers, or resource people. They know which colleagues they can depend on for what. It is not unusual for star teachers to have a support network of teachers from several schools so that there is a critical mass. Such support networks counteract burnout by offering mutual support and by generating activities that provide ideas and sustenance to the group members. A support network is a more powerful antidote for burnout than individual teachers left to their own devices who can only talk over their problems with a spouse or a priest. Looking to renewal from a college course is also less satisfactory than the personal support of other teachers facing similar problems in the same bureaucracy.

There are many other bureaucracies besides schools. Our society is replete with governmental organizations and private companies whose structures work against the clients rather than for them. Successful people in all walks of life deal with the mid-range function described here. For this reason, teachers who have been successful in other careers are more likely to be able to survive in dysfunctional school districts than those who have never worked for sustained periods in other fields. It is unfortunate for the children and youth in the major urban school districts that only stars and a few others are capable of performing this function. Students not only need good teachers, but teachers who will stay. The naïve idealism that schools should not be organized and operated as dysfunctional bureaucracies prevents many teachers—and those who prepare them—from learning to perform this extremely vital set of functions.

N. Fallibility

When teachers are asked, "Do you ever make mistakes?" they answer, "Of course, I'm only human. Everyone makes mistakes!" The difference between stars and quitter/failures is in the nature of the mistakes they recognize and own up to. Quitter/failures talk about misspelling a word or getting an answer wrong in an arithmetic problem. They might admit to transcribing a wrong grade onto a report card. Essentially, they are admitting to slips, typos, and inadvertent minor errors. Stars, on the other hand, confess to serious errors which involve breaking trust: e.g. misjudging a child in some important way, blaming or publicly embarrassing a student for something. Although they know their children quite well, they confess errors of occasionally rushing to judgment too quickly without getting all the facts about a particular incident. Although their errors of judgment are rare, stars are willing to confess to serious lapses which may result in breaking trust with a child. Quitter/ failures simply cannot own up to anything that is a serious mistake involving relationships with their students, parents or school staff.

Another discriminating factor between the two groups is what they do after committing a mistake. How do they correct them? Quitter/failures talk only about minor slips so that correcting such mistakes is no trouble at all. For stars, who are willing to confess to serious misjudgments that endanger the rapport and trust they have established with children, correcting mistakes is messy and takes some doing. Stars are aware, for example, that if they criticize, blame, or accuse a child publicly they must apologize and rectify the situation publicly. They do not criticize in public and apologize in private.

STAR TEACHERS

When quitter/failures admit to blaming the wrong child for something they find it difficult if not impossible to apologize under any conditions. The following dialogue captures quitter/failure ideology and behavior.

Questioner: Imagine that you have a student named Franklin who has been taking things from his neighbors desks all year. Is it possible you might have a child like this in your class?

Respondent: Yes.

Questioner: One day a child sitting next to Franklin reports something missing. You ask Franklin in front of the whole class to return the missing item. Later on another child confesses. What would you do?

Respondent: I'd take Franklin aside and explain to him that I misjudged him this time because he's always taking things. I'd want him to understand that if he wasn't continually misbehaving I wouldn't have misjudged him.

Questioner: You'd talk to him privately.

Respondent: Yes.

Questioner: Would you apologize?

Respondent: I might or might not use the word "apologize", but I would indicate I was sorry about misjudging him. The important thing for Franklin to understand is that his behavior all year is the reason I accused him.

This reluctance to admit to serious errors, especially in the presence of children, is typical of teachers who have a problem owning mistakes. They appear to be fearful of admitting mistakes because they believe they will lose stature in the eyes of the children. Actually, the exact reverse is true. In some cases, they are unwilling to admit mistakes because they believe that intelligent, competent professionals never make any. Whatever the cause of their reluctance, they rarely admit to serious mistakes and if they do, they never correct them publicly. As in the dialogue above, they do not see the need to publicly correct mistakes made in public. When they do speak to a child they have misjudged they are likely to dig an even deeper hole and point to the child's past misdeeds as the cause of their mistake. In some cases, quitter/failures will take the position that they will not commit any mistakes at all! After agreeing that everyone makes mistakes and that it is only human to do so, they may sit quietly for several seconds thinking over the contradiction in their responses. They are likely to conclude the dialogue with: "I know I will make some mistakes, I just can't think of any right now." If given a sufficiently long period of time they may finally offer a verbal typo. "Oh, I suppose I might mispronounce one of those funny names, you know." When asked what they would do about such a mistake they respond, "Oh just go on and pretend it never happened." Admitting to mistakes is very, very hard for them.

This mid-range function is highly predictive of teacher's future classroom behavior. Individuals who cannot recognize, admit, or abide mistakes in themselves are not likely to be tolerant of others' mistakes. An individual who believes that s/he is somehow a lesser person or has been diminished by making a mistake is very likely to feel this way about others. Teaching is the worst possible job for such a person! Imagine trying to learn math, science or language from someone who is annoyed by mistakes or puts a negative value on trying and failing. Children not only make mistakes all the time in the course of their learning but also commit serious errors in their relationships with others. It is in the nature of life in the classroom for mistakes to be a typical and recurring condition.

As in all the previous mid-range functions, fallibility is a combination of stars' ideology and their practice. Because they hold a set of beliefs about the naturalness of fallibility, they are led to behave in human and humane ways when mistakes occur. On a behavioral level teacher and pupil mistakes are often treated humorously. Mistakes are even celebrated as an example of how adults as well as children all need to do better. Stars frequently model the acceptance of mistakes and on occasion use it as a teachable moment.

Consider the following example.

A star second grade teacher was making certain that all the children in his class knew their addresses and phone numbers and could write them. The idea was that this was a safety need should they become lost in the city. On checking their papers one of the brightest girls in the class whispered to him, "I can't write the name of the street I live on." In a loud voice the teacher made the child's confession public and said, "Trinki can't write her

189

address. I am really surprised. This is terrible! Trinki, tell me the street you live on and I will write it down on the blackboard and you can copy it down and learn it. Now, where do you live?" If the teacher had checked the class register he would have seen that Trinki lived on a street with a long Native American name (Aneskumonnica). Instead, he embarrassed Trinki first, and then waited at the blackboard to write out the correct spelling. When Trinki told him the name he was embarrassed because he couldn't spell it either. He immediately apologized profusely to Trinki in front of the class and then enlisted the help of the class. This became an interesting activity because the street turned out to be only one block long and the street sign was missing. Some children checked with neighbors, some asked at the post office and the teacher checked the school records. This turned up three different spellings. The teacher kept referring back to his mistake every time a child came up with another spelling. For the rest of the year the teacher found appropriate occasions to remind the children of his mistake and model more reasonable behavior. For example, if a child answered too quickly, or didn't check his work, or laughed at another child's answer, the teacher would say, "Is this really true or are we repeating my mistake? Is this another Aneskumonnica? Everyone would laugh and recheck their papers.

The importance of fallibility cannot be overstated. In urban schools serving diverse children in urban poverty, student interactions become extremely competitive beginning in third grade, especially for males. It is common to see children working at the blackboard or giving answers orally to be derided by catcalls and epithets from fellow students. The climate the teacher has established in these classrooms is that mistakes are not supposed to happen—that they are a sign of weakness or stupidity. The climate is such that when a student makes a mistake it becomes an opportunity for the others to demonstrate superiority. These street values can only be changed by teachers who consciously and actively teach children that we all make mistakes and that we all learn from them. The child so fearful of being wrong doesn't try and once trying stops, learning stops. The surest way to teach children and youth to accept their own fallibility is to have teachers who can accept theirs.

Chapter XIV
Commom Questions Asked of Star Teachers

There are "hot issues" that are frequently asked about the ideology of star teachers which are not directly covered in describing their mid-range functions. In this section some of the most common problems faced by classroom teachers are discussed in terms of how stars deal with them.

Discipline

Stars do not spend much time or effort on discipline. They usually have three or four rules which they establish at the beginning of each year. They are not fixated with this issue as their highest priority or as even a major concern. On a list of the things they care about most, discipline may not appear at all! This is not to say that they don't face the same horrendous management issues that all teachers deal with in poverty schools, including children facing death threats, being assaulted, or living in unsafe conditions. The fact that they live with these problems daily still does not make discipline their major concern. Stars' ability to relate to the children puts them on the same side as the students rather than making them adversaries. The inability of quitter/failures to relate to their students makes any management system they try ineffective and explains why discipline and classroom control remains their top concern regardless of how long they teach.

There are several reasons why stars view discipline as they do. First, they believe and accept the fact that problems will always be part of the teacher's job. They know that many of their youngsters are growing up in less than ideal conditions and bring their problems to school with them. They know many youngsters have health issues. Others suffer from nutrition problems and various forms of physical and emotional abuse. As children become teenagers there is strong peer pressure exerted against trying to be successful in school. Stars also know they may have as many as six or seven youngsters with handicapping conditions in their classrooms as well as several children who are homeless. In my city approximately 8,000 students are homeless. In short, stars recognize and accept the fact that their students live with a wide range of negative conditions which interfere with learning. They need teachers who engage them in learning and help them achieve in spite of these negative conditions. If problems were not an expected part of the job, then teaching would simply be a matter of explaining stuff, making assignments and marking the papers of children who happily comply with directions—and anyone could do it.

Traditional teacher training is counter productive for those who would teach diverse children in poverty since it leads them to perceive a substantial number, even a majority, of their students as abnormal in some way. Emotionally disturbed, cognitively disabled, learning disabled and other labels are catch-all categories that essentially identify minority children the teachers are unable to relate to. The children need teachers who can do more than give them directions and monitor compliance. Quitter/failure teachers believe that their preservice training did not prepare them to deal with the children they would be expected to teach—and they are correct. They were selected and prepared to teach only children who are not dependent on their teachers for what they learn; that is, children whose life conditions and support networks guarantee their success in school regardless of how competent their teachers are. To the extent that children are dependent on teachers for what they learn they are disadvantaged because traditional teacher training selects and prepares individuals to perceive diverse children in poverty as "problems" who shouldn't be in their classrooms.

The second reason stars view discipline as less than a major issue is that they spend so little time on it. They are proactive disciplinarians. Their normal teaching style involves much individual interaction with students. They observe and study their students. This enables stars to anticipate, prevent and ward off many problems. The information stars constantly gain from children makes it easier to plan for what they will do in advance and to deal with disciplinary or emergency situations if they arise. It is unlikely that students will lash out at teachers who have established relationships with them, and who have demonstrated respect and caring. It is easier and more likely students will make themselves problems to strangers or people they do not respect. What stars do is establish working relationships with children around the learning activities of the classroom. They do not try to develop personal relationships with youngsters around discipline problems after such problems arise. Stars are able to spend so little time on discipline because they have invested so much of their time and effort creating interesting learning activities that enable them to build caring relationships with each of their children.

A third reason stars do not perceive discipline as a major issue is that they expect a range of achievement levels in their classrooms in the same way they expect a range of behaviors. They do not begin with the quitter/ failure's assumption that their classes should be comprised of a homogenous ability group, all of whom are on or near grade level. They don't create discipline problems by assigning tasks the students perceive as too easy (a sign of disrespect) or impossible to complete (a source of frustration). By using differential assignments, stars provide meaningful work to everyone. In the rooms of quitter/failures there is only one assignment for everyone and the frustrations of those who need more advanced work and those who need more basic skills are manifested in misbehavior.

Fourth, stars do not escalate problems. What they say and physically communicate is that whatever problems arise are solvable and solvable quickly. Discipline experts, regardless of the particular systems they advocate, are unanimous in their agreement that teachers cause most of their own classroom problems and then escalate them further rather than defuse them. Stars do not respond to students and to problem situations as if their primary function is deciding guilt or innocence and meting out justice. Teachers who view themselves as judge/prosecutors of student misbehavior inevitably escalate discipline problems and are doomed to fail. Stars' primary concern is not finding the best punishment for misbehavior but identifying the motivation of the child creating the problem. Stars believe they have a responsibility to help children overcome whatever is interfering with their ability to perform and get along with others. They do not perceive of the children as perpetrators. This is a significant difference: stars seek ways of treating the causes of misbehavior and quitter/failures seek appropriate punishments for misbehavior. The teacher who thinks in terms of punishments as the cures for misbehavior will inevitably escalate discipline problems further.

Fifth, stars use some form of logical consequences to guide their children in recognizing and dealing with misbehavior in the classroom. They teach the children, to see that whatever they do will generate a result that they must deal with in future. This approach was developed by Rudolph Dreikurs whose theory of classroom discipline is based on the teacher first determining the motive for a child's misbehavior. Dreikurs proposed only four student motives: the need for attention, power, revenge and avoidance of failure. In this approach the teacher stops responding to discipline with a set of fixed, preset punishments and responds to each child in terms of his/her specific motive for misbehaving. After the teacher decides which of the four causes is motivating the child to misbehave, she makes the most appropriate response to that motive. For example, if a child is vying with the teacher for control of the classroom it is more appropriate to make him a leader of some activity than a child whose motive is to avoid failure.

In creating the Star Classroom Management Protocol, I have identified a pool of fifty positive teacher responses which are triggered by one of these four student motives. This is an interactive computer exercise in which teachers practice responding quickly to children who are misbehaving for one of the four reasons cited. What this means in practice is that star teachers do not make the same responses to all students for all misbehaviors. Pat teacher responses such as putting a check next to a child's name, or sending him out of the room, or calling home are not appropriate responses for all children in all situations. Indeed, it is unlikely they are ever effective responses for any misdeed. Until the teacher learns the child's motive and makes an appropriate, positive response to the motivation for the misbehavior it will continue and worsen. Stars do not all use Dreikurs' four categories, but they inevitably use a similar system of logical consequences. They act only in terms of the most appropriate teacher response to a particular child, after they determine his motive. They never respond as if there is a universally correct teacher response to a child's misbehavior without first knowing that child's motivation.

Thus far, several reasons have been offered for why stars do not regard discipline as their major problem or even a high priority. They expect problems as part of their normal workload. They build strong personal relationships with children around learning tasks and do not leave the process of relating to a child until after a serious problem arises. They expect and plan for wide differences in achievement in the same class and anticipate working with many children below grade level. Their assignments account for these differences. They do not escalate problems by misperceiving their role to be an arbiter of punishments. They respond to a student's misbehavior in terms of the particular student's need and thereby change his/her motive for misbehaving. They act with confidence in a relaxed professional manner rather than present a frenzied, harried or authoritarian image to their students. Teachers who lack self-confidence and self-esteem cannot build self-confidence and self-esteem in others. "It takes somebodys to make somebody. Nobodys don't make somebodys."

These are not rules for becoming a great disciplinarian, rather an analysis of how stars' perception of their role differentiates them from other teachers. Stars deal with children and youth who face the same range of horrendous life problems as all teachers who work with youngsters growing up in poverty. The major difference between stars and other teachers is that most others— particularly quitter/failures—perceive of discipline as an issue separate from teaching. They see discipline as a set of procedures that must be put in place before learning can occur and do not understand that discipline problems emanate from the way they are teaching. If they get to know children in any depth at all, it is after undesirable events have occurred...and not always then. Stars do the reverse. They establish in-depth caring relationships in the course of their day-to-day teaching activities and avoid, deflect or defuse problems that would inevitably arise if such rapport had not been developed. They know this will not forestall all problems, but it will make their work manageable. The fact that they expect and plan for problems gives them a different perspective from other teachers. Again, this difference is between treating discipline as a prior condition requiring a separate set of controls apart from how learning activities are pursued, versus offering interesting learning activities which have the effect of involving and controlling student behavior. When students are involved in an activity they discipline themselves. Unfortunately most teachers who work with diverse children in poverty never learn this. If they did, their most pressing question would change from "How do I control them?" to "How do I involve them?"

Most teachers learn, some quickly others eventually, that "Ten Easy Steps to Discipline" will not be useful to them, or resolve their classroom problems, or cut down on the stress felt by their children and themselves. What they are less likely to understand is that their effectiveness in discipline is a function of their ability to relate to the children and hook them on learning. Discipline is not a set of prior conditions or problems that must be resolved before teaching can occur. It is a consequence, a result, an outcome of teachers and students who respect and care about each other doing interesting things together.

A final caveat is in order. Quitter/failure teachers frequently state, "With more than thirty students in a room it is impossible to learn and use all this knowledge about individual kids." This rationalization neglects the facts. These same teachers spend endless hours during and after school with misbehaving students, parents, principals and others after incidents have occurred. The investment in teacher time would have been much less if made beforehand. Poor teachers spend more time on after-the-fact discipline than stars spend on finding interesting things for children to learn and do. How the teacher spends her time is not a function of objectively how much time she has, but a question of how she believes effective classroom management is achieved.

Punishment

Twenty-two state legislatures have explicitly made corporal punishment legal. In eight other states the legislatures have left to local school districts the decision of whether or not to use the practice. In a majority of states, therefore, beating the client is considered a method of teaching. In contrast, every European country has outlawed corporal punishment. Indeed, with the exception of Great Britain, they have made it illegal for parents to hit or spank their own children and define the practice as abuse. The notion that American teachers would have this legal right is beyond the comprehension of people in civilized societies. The fact that corporal punishment still exists in a majority of states is very revealing about the public perception of the goals of schooling, the role of the teacher and how people believe learning takes place.

The State of Texas leads the nation every year in the number of corporal punishments administered by teachers and typically reports over 500,000 annually. It is reasonable to assume that many more incidents go unreported than are recorded because every state requires that numerous forms be completed and that the spanking must be done in front of a witness on the school staff. The question for teachers is simple, "Can one practice a 'profession' by beating the client?"

Star teachers do not engage in corporal punishment, use very few punishments and do not think in terms of punishments. They are also not proponents of behavior modification and as quickly as possible try to move away from using external rewards at all. Their goal is move children to seek intrinsic rewards for learning. Star teachers know they cannot control all their students' reactions and perceptions—let alone all their drives. They do not see themselves as all powerful reinforcers, extinguishers, shapers, or controllers of children's behavior in the same way as an experimental psychologist running laboratory rats. Behavior modification is an ideal way to train animals to perform all sorts of tasks in response to rewards of food and water. It cannot be used to teach human beings to pursue learning for its intrinsic value. Star teachers see their role as coaching and providing help. They believe their role is to encourage students to want to do the work for the satisfaction that will be derived from being successful at that work. They do not see themselves monitoring a menu of extrinsic rewards. Stars also perceive of punishments as examples of extrinsic controls. The fact that stars use ordinary language rather than psychological jargon reflects their perception that they are human beings interacting with other human beings and not scientists controlling the behavior of others. They even tend to shy away from the term motivation and use everyday words such as interest, involvement, participation and engagement. Stars know and accept the reality that ultimately they cannot force anyone to learn. They see their job as eliciting and guiding it.

The basic reason stars do not rely on punishment is that it doesn't work. The fact that it is the same youngsters who are punished over and over demonstrates that it is a failed strategy for stamping out misbehavior or generating desirable behavior. Regardless of the type of punishments, how administered, by whom and under what conditions, it doesn't cause interest or achievement to improve. Teachers who buy into punishment simply escalate problems in sequence: i.e. warn, withdraw a privilege, administer a negative consequence, remove, suspend and finally expel. Not only are such procedures ineffective, but the number of at-risk, disruptive and failing students is skyrocketing in response to teachers using more and more punishments. Nowhere is the failure of this theory more evident than among adolescents. The rewards which adolescents receive from their peers for non-compliance and disruption (approval and acceptance) are more infinitely more powerful than any of the teacher's or school's punishments.

Meting out punishments is the last refuge of those who believe they have the power to compel reluctant learners to shape up and make people learn. There can be no masking this essentially authoritarian philosophy. Teachers who use escalating punishments are assuming they can force people to comply and that by such coerced obedience they can make students learn. Children sense from the earliest ages, even before they can fully comprehend what is fully happening to them, that they must fight for their freedom against external control over their minds, bodies and spirits. Most children in poverty schools become passive resisters after the primary grades and thereafter "protect" themselves from becoming fully involved in school. They comply outwardly but resist inwardly. As a result, the thirteen years they spend in school following directions and avoiding punishments develops only a fraction of their potential. It does not create self-directed learners.

Not all children in poverty respond passively to the authoritarianism of teachers who see punishment as educative. As they grow in size many fight back directly. In so doing they are saying in effect, "You can't make me do anything. Your punishments are nothing to me. I have more power than you to decide what I will and will not do." Teachers who believe that escalating punishments will cure students' apathy or misbehavior ignore the evidence they see acted out before them everyday. Those being punished are not transformed. The most reasonable conclusion for explaining this phenomenon is that the culture of the school and the ideology of the teachers lock them into repeating failed strategies of disciplinary punishments over and over. What are we to assume about people who insist on failing in the same old ways? In two separate studies, I analyzed the work of teachers in a prison high school. The incarcerated students were required to attend school everyday. The teachers had rewards and punishments which were more powerful than teachers in regular high schools including: water, food, privacy, cigarettes, sleep, and even time added or subtracted from an inmate's sentence. Most of the students were apathetic, quiet and detached. They appeared to learn a few basic things, but none became either avid readers or auto mechanics. At best, they demonstrated a few low level skills while incarcerated. Even when the teachers had these very powerful rewards and punishments at their disposal, the students successfully resisted being forced to learn. They complied outwardly but internalized little or nothing. Upon release none finished high school. A few passed GED's by aged thirty. A majority returned to prison. When I share this example with teachers they do not conclude that a system of escalating powerful punishments fails to create students who will want to learn. The reaction of most teachers to these studies is envy. They believe that if they had access to the powerful rewards and punishments of the teachers in the prison high school that they would be more effective with their students. In effect, they buy into the punishment model and just feel handicapped by not having sufficiently powerful ones. What they seem to be searching for is a surefire set of increasingly powerful rewards and punishments which could be dispensed first, second and third to compel student learning. Stars do not fantasize about such a coercive system. They do not believe that punishment can be educative. They use punishment as a last resort and recognize that when they do, it is a failure on their part, i.e. they have given up on a youngster, at least for the time being. In the high schools in my city, sixty-five percent of the students are suspended at least once during the year and in the middle schools fifty percent of the students are suspended at least once during the year. Star teachers go through a whole year in these schools working with the very same students and never suspend anyone.

The question of who is being punished for what must also be faced. Are offending students punishing themselves, other students, or the teachers? Teachers are frequently unaware of how some students push them into administering punishments only to prove that they are controlling the teacher's behavior. In a very real sense, eliciting punishments can be quite rewarding for many students. It takes the focus off learning, where the teacher is in charge and makes the issue one of "who is in control of the class's attention"? Once the contest is for control over the class's attention, the student will always win if s/he is willing to bear the consequences. No punishment can force him/her to learn anything. Many students derive great satisfaction from yanking the teacher's punishment chain, especially teachers with whom they have not connected.

Stars create a community in their classrooms which then sets up the norms of expected behavior. In these rooms discipline is no longer a matter between the teacher and the offender. It is a matter of justice and equity between the individual and the rest of the class. The class is somehow disturbed or prevented from working. The class recognizes offenses and what needs to be done. The effective teacher in a classroom community is, in a very real sense, the representative of the group. This does not mean that the teacher uses the group to ostracize or alienate youngsters who are very likely to be in need of greater group acceptance, support, or recognition. It does mean that the effective teacher knows that it is the teacher's role to implement an agreed-upon standard. Indeed, if left to their own devices, children will frequently advocate inappropriately severe consequences. The teacher is needed to mitigate such harsh justice. At other times, star teachers involve the group in judging the fairness of some decision they have made. Star teachers prepare their students for this role of making judgments about their own behavior and the behavior of their peers. They begin in September when the students are expecting the teacher to be the sole arbiter of justice. Gradually, as a community is created in the classroom, the teacher moves more and more decisions about behavior from ones she makes to decisions made with the students. By the year's end, in a classroom that has become a community, most of the decisions will be made by the students themselves. Rational authority is self eliminating.

Homework

Star teachers do not assign homework in the traditional sense,"Do page fifty-eight in the arithmetic book." They create assignments that will interest and be relevant in the same way they would if these were in-class assignments. Homework is planned with children and grows out of classroom activities. In order to be effective, homework must put the students in the role of researcher who finds out things that make him/her an expert who can come back to class and share what has been learned. This provides an opportunity for further teacher encouragement and the cycle continues. Examples of such homework include interviewing resource people, finding out how something in the community works, constructing something, conducting an experiment that can only be done out of school (such as testing a lawn for lead content), or finishing a piece of writing.

Typically, homework is drill and kill; i.e. skills that the teacher has failed to teach during school hours. Then parents, without teaching credentials, are asked to teach the skills teachers have failed to teach. Not only quitter/ failures, but most teachers, see the parent's role as teaching—and teaching so effectively that the children who are behind in basic skills will be caught up by doing homework with their parents. Most parents in poverty, on the other hand, expect the teachers who are paid much more than they are to do their jobs more effectively. When urban teachers are asked about parents they complain, "I never see hardly any." When asked what they would like of parents they say "Help their kids with homework!" or "Come into the school and tutor kids who are behind." Parents do not come for a variety of reasons. They know they will merely hear more complaints about their children from teachers—teachers who they believe they are the cause of their child's poor achievement or behavior. They resent being held accountable for their children's learning when they believe the schools and teachers should be held accountable. Others may be working several jobs and simply not have the time.

Star teachers are not trapped in this morass. Their homework is not a routine of drill, neither is it an attempt to transfer the failure the teacher has experienced to the parents. Each assignment is special and meets the same level of interest and meaningfulness as an in-class activity. Homework in stars' rooms is not merely checked off or graded; it is shared. The question, "Did you do your homework?" is replaced by giving children opportunities to share and explain what they have accomplished and learned. Nothing is ever sent home as homework that the teacher is unsure the child can do independently in the hope that someone at home will do better at teaching it than the teacher has.

STAR TEACHERS

Parental Relations

Star teachers describe parental support in terms of parents providing safety, sleep, nutrition, health care and opportunities to learn from community activities. There are of course many parents who don't or can't provide these basics. Some are adolescents themselves. Others have never experienced success in school and feel uneasy about using themselves as models. While it is possible to find parents who hurt their children by abuse and neglect, star teachers act on the belief that parents love their children deeply and would like to help them succeed. Stars' relationship with parents is one of shared responsibility. They make home visits and if parents are uncomfortable about this they meet them in a neighborhood McDonald's®. The teacher's purpose for parental contact is to share positive things about their work and for learning more about their out-of-school lives in order to be more able to interest them in their studies. When, and if, there are negative things to communicate, the groundwork of a respectful relationship with parents has been laid. Stars relate to parents in poverty in the same way they would relate to wealthy parents and the school was a prestigious private one...with respect and by listening to the aspirations of the parents for their children.

In failing schools parents are treated as if they shouldn't be there and are an unnecessary nuisance. They are also treated as if the role of the school is to explain things to them, rather than to seek their input and ideas. This is especially true for schools serving Latino populations where the school makes a lack of English synonymous with stupidity. Frequently the bilingual aide helps the parents fill out forms and gives directions on how to comply with the school rules. The schools policies and regulations are treated as inviolate. They are not subject to being justified or amended as in schools serving advantaged children where the parents are not only listened to but heard. Parents in urban districts are made to feel helpless by the ways in which schools and teachers present problems to them. They feel denigrated by the way in which schools and teachers communicate with them and the content of those communications. In my city there are 167 schools and parents have the legal right to transfer their children out of failing schools. The parent manual on how to sequence that in a district with 89,000 students there are fewer than a few hundred student actually affect a transfer is so complex and involves so many steps to be completed in transfers a year. Compounding this "communication" problem is the annual designation of schools that are failing. One year there were fifty-eight schools officially designated as failing. The school system informed the parents of 45,000 students, as required by law, that they had the right to transfer their children out of these failing schools. The parents were not informed which schools were not failing. Neither were they informed whether there were any vacancies in the more successful schools. As a result of such parental "communication", less than 500 of the 45,000 children had parents with the know-how to get them transferred— and those parents might well have transferred their children into another failing school or one not much better than the one they just left. If this level of "communication" occurred in a suburban or small town school district, the school board would risk being recalled and the superintendent might well be dismissed.

Quitter/failures blame the parents. In former times they might also have blamed the hereditary that produced low I.Q's. In today's politically correct world, quitter/failures blame the poor living conditions and life experiences of children in poverty. In either case the victim, his family and his ethnicity is blamed for the schools' and teachers' inability to produce effective learners. The voices of failure/quitter teachers are loud and clear: "What do you want from me? I'm not a social worker or a nurse!"

Stars perceive of parents and caregivers as partners not as a substitute teachers. Stars treat parents with respect by not only listening but by hearing them. They believe they are like other parents and want the very best for their children. Stars create this working partnership by the way they communicate and by what they communicate. Parents quickly see that star teachers really care about their children and are working very hard to increase their learning. Parents are impressed by the time teachers take to learn more about their children, to use what they find out to make learning more interesting and relevant, and by the ways in which the teachers enable children to show off to parents all that they have accomplished in school. Star teachers frequently hold fairs, plays, exhibitions, fiestas and other culminating activities which put parents in the position of being able to take pride in their children's accomplishments. Finally, stars don't pander to parents and automatically accede to every request. Some parents believe they can give a teacher permission to use corporal punishment. Stars live out the philosophy, "What the wisest best parents want for their children, the community should want for all its children."

Achievement Tests

Stars know that tests mandated by the state and local districts are not going away. If anything, there will be more of them in future. Testing is a windmill they don't waste energy tilting at. They do not believe in any form of norm-referenced tests because their ideology tells them that knowledge is not a commodity that increases in value because others have less of it. They do not support assessment for the purpose of producing winners and losers. Stars also question competency based tests because there are always issues of who decided on the competencies and whether the competencies being assessed represent an adequate sample of the knowledge in the particular field of study. In spite of all their misgivings, however, stars accept that testing will continue to be an inevitable fact of life in schools, especially in urban schools dependent on federal and state grants. Their stance can best be described as accepting the reality of tests, without succumbing and teaching to the tests. This position requires demonstrating a great deal of confidence in sticking to their ideology. Stars believe that their teaching methods are so powerful that they can maintain their integrity by continuing to use methods that involve students in thematic and project teaching and not lapse into the drill and kill of teaching for the test. Stars are able to lead youngsters to not only high scores on the mandated tests, but to learning important subject matter at advanced levels. In practice this means that stars do not make the tests the curriculum. They have confidence in their ability to get their students to demonstrate higher achievement as a result of learning the stated curriculum rather than just receiving test preparation. Quitter/failures focus on the tests and the kind of items tested for. They teach to the tests, become obsessed by the tests and yet, their students do not demonstrate satisfactory achievement. In a very real sense, by ignoring the tests and teaching the curriculum in the most relevant ways, stars do what the test makers would expect of effective good teachers. It is the stars' ideology that gives them the confidence to act on their beliefs and commitments and to stick with best practices that will engender the greatest student interest and involvement.

In a research-demonstration of this belief that good teachers do not have to teach for the test, I worked with a group of teachers in an elementary school in Spring Branch, Texas. In this Houston area school serving Mexican children in extreme poverty, the school had to be reconstituted. As a result, I was able to use the mid-range functions described in this volume to select the entire staff. Many were veteran teachers, others were beginners. They all passed the interview and a few responded at the level of stars. I was able to convince them that if they taught according to their ideology the tests would take care of themselves. The teachers agreed to try and did their usual teaching, which included diverse methods and great reliance on thematic units. No teacher lapsed into drill and kill on test-like items. In one year this school moved from the lowest achieving school in the district to among the three highest. This demonstration was replicated with a faculty selected by my interview in Highgate Heights, a public elementary school in Buffalo, New York serving African American students in poverty. Star teachers do not let the need for mandated testing interfere with what they know to be effective instruction.

Chapter XV
Gentle Teaching in a Violent Society

Approximately 160,000 crimes are committed everyday in schools. Over half a million attacks, shakedowns and robberies occur in secondary schools in one month. Over three million incidents of assault, rape, robbery and theft occur on school property annually. The New York City Schools has the ninth largest police force in the country. Dade County, Florida budgets over $16,000,000 per year for security. In major urban districts teachers are willing to bargain for two items above increased salary: health coverage and safety.

In many urban communities more than twenty-five percent of the youngsters have witnessed a murder and seventy-five percent know someone who has been shot. Ten percent of children treated in hospitals have witnessed a stabbing or shooting before the age of six. In my own relatively small city, 119 school age children were murdered in the last three years. Across the nation, approximately 1,000 teachers are threatened daily with bodily harm.

American society is violent, the urban neighborhoods are violent and the schools reflect this violence. Not very far beneath the surface of all urban schools is the potential for unleashing uncontrollable violence. Teachers who really understand the constant threat and horrific consequences of school violence will be sufficiently on-guard to deflect or prevent it. The potential for violence smolders in many of the youngsters and only teachers who see the deep frustration and anger children carry into the school building with them will be sufficiently sensitive to avoid setting it off. Urban teachers know that preventing violence is an integral part of their legitimate work; the more effective they are at empowering youngsters, the less violence they will engender. The less effective they are at relating to students in positive, supportive ways, the more violence they will cause.

Star Teachers

Feelings of deep frustration are the major characteristic of both adults and children who grow up and experience urban poverty. The inevitable result of frustration is aggression. For many, it is expressed as violence toward others. For others, it is turned inward and expressed in the multiple ways people demonstrate a reckless abandon for their own bodies, including suicide.

The attitudes with which most poor children begin school are remarkably positive given their life experiences. Not being certain of which adults they can trust, living in neighborhoods where violence is common, surrounded by friends and family not getting the services they are entitled to, the children still come to school with high expectations for how they will be treated. It is incumbent on schools to offer them more than a new set of adults who are overly directive and authoritarian.

The ideology of star teachers regarding violence and what they can do about it is both realistic and hopeful. Their first goal is to not make matters worse. Their second goal is to create a classroom climate in which children succeed and relate to one another in ways not determined by the threat of force and coercion. Stars work toward this goal using various forms of gentle teaching.

Teachers in schools serving children in poverty have no choice other than gentle teaching. Beyond kindergarten and the first few grades, the teachers can no longer physically control their students with external sanctions and fear. For teachers to believe and act as if they have the means to force students to learn, or even comply, is a dangerous myth that can make poor schools as coercive and violent as the neighborhoods outside the school. Children who grow up in neighborhoods where they are socialized to deal with violence, abuse and even death will not be readily cowed into submission by punishments such as a time-out room or the threat of suspension and expulsion. As children mature the harshest punishments available to schools and teachers can be ignored and even laughed at by students. Why then do school officials and teachers continue to pretend they can coerce, force, insist upon, demand, require, or see to it that the children can be made to comply and learn? The answers that can explain this phenomenon are: 1) educators do not know viable alternatives to directive, coercive teaching; 2) the people who choose to become teachers are have a need to demonstrate power and control over others; 3) programs of teacher preparation do not teach specific strategies for dealing with the life experiences of diverse children in poverty; and 4) the conditions of work in schools limit teachers to replicating failed strategies harder and with greater energy.

Stars realize very quickly that they can only succeed by getting off the power theme. Ultimately, each student is in control of what and how much s/he learns. "Make" is the critical word here. In failing schools the staff is looking for ways to "make" students learn. The students define good teachers as those who "made" me learn. In contrast, stars define their objective as making the student want to learn. How is this related to school violence? Empowering students in decision-making and engaging them in learning activities transforms a violent school into one with only an occasional instance of violence. There is no debate about this point among knowledgeable educators. Teachers who believe they must dominate children and youth in poverty in order to teach them are doomed to fail. Even worse, they raise the levels of frustration among students getting bigger and stronger who they pass on to the next grade. Following are some of the gentle teaching strategies used by star teachers.

• "Covering" material without first generating student interest and involvement is a waste of time and does not lead to learning. Subject matter must be connected with students, not used to dominate them or prove they are incapable of learning difficult ideas.

• Shame or humiliation is an effective means of cutting down on student effort and guaranteed to prevent a positive relationship between teacher and student.

• Shouting, critical lecturing and moralizing effectively demonstrate to students that the teacher is out of control and at a loss for how to proceed.

• Increasing the severity of punishments is an effective means of escalating minor problems into major ones and changing short term problems into persisting ones.

• Hearing rather than listening and then using student's ideas has a powerful, positive impact on student learning.

• Students are likely to imitate and replicate teachers who model positive interactions with other adults in the school.

• Showing respect for student opinions with which they disagree has a powerful effect on the particular student who has the differing opinion and an even greater impact on the class observing this behavior.

• Getting students to express their feelings is an indicator of good teaching. Accepting students' feelings is an indicator of high quality teaching.

• Making referrals to appropriate people who can help an abused, sick, or homeless child is an important way in which teachers demonstrate caring and empathy.

• Rewarding students who resolve differences by means other than violence or coercion is of critical importance. Defining adults who use peaceful means to resolve differences as heroes, has an important influence on students.

• Repeated failure is never educative and inevitably leads to not trying. Only success experiences can lead to increased student effort.

• Every student is talented, or has a potentially exceptional proclivity to achieve something at a high level. The effective teacher is always on the hunt for each student's secret talent or bent.

• Stars never confront anyone publicly. They defuse, deflect, sidestep, and redirect all challenges to teacher authority.

• Teachers who create a community in the classroom not only have few, if any, management problems, but actually enjoy interacting with the very students other teachers cannot manage.

• Effective teachers respect student privacy. They never ask for private information in public.

• Demonstrating respect for parents in the presence of their children and demonstrating respect for children in the presence of their parents has a great positive impact on everyone's subsequent behavior.

• Legitimizing student aggression and even the urge to fight by having heated debates regarding issues in science, social studies and other subject matters is a star teacher strategy.

These behaviors do not guarantee that all violence will be kept out of the school. But the effect of these gentle, respectful teaching behaviors will be to significantly cut down on the number of serious disruptions and will de-escalate most of the others.

Star teachers see their job as helping to create safe havens where, for a good part of everyday, the violence of our society does not intrude and children can be free from fear. Quitter/failure teachers do not have this concept of their role. They believe that violence should never be present in a school, and therefore, it should not be part of their job to have to plan for or deal with it. Because of these opposing views, stars see the world as it is and quitter/failures see it in terms of some idealized fantasy. As with the mid-range functions this leads the two groups to perform entirely different jobs as teachers. Stars engage in gentle teaching aimed at making learning intrinsic and holding students accountable while quitter/failures seek to implement a directive, authoritarian model the youngsters are bound to resist and overcome.

The strength of star teachers is unrelated to their physical makeup. Self confidence and the strength to function peacefully in volatile and potentially violent situations is an inner strength. A frail, elderly female middle school teacher might be effective with the very same difficult students who drive a male, macho ex-football player to resign. The willingness and ability to share authority with children and youth who most people are unwilling to trust requires strength of character and is a star attribute.

211

Chapter XVI
Only Decent People Should Teach

By this time my assumptions should be clear. The selection of teachers is infinitely more important than the nature of their training. What colleges and universities cannot teach is the ability to relate to diverse children in poverty and to persist at a job in a failing bureaucracy organized for the benefit of the adults and against the best educational interests of the children. Learning subject matter content and pedagogical content in colleges and universities can be readily achieved, but the ideology and mid-range functions described in this volume cannot. What this means in the real world, is that after the teacher has demonstrated the ability to relate and survive, how much she knows becomes of critical importance, but content knowledge by itself predicts quitter/failures. As I reflect on the last half century of preparing teachers on-the-job I cannot recall a single instance in which a teacher who could relate to the children failed, or a case in which a teacher who could not relate succeeded. Content can be learned but these relationship skills and their undergirding ideology cannot. If knowledge of content and pedagogy were the best criteria for predicting teacher effectiveness, then faculty in the math departments of universities, or faculty in the schools of education, could teach effectively for sustained periods in urban middle schools. We recognize such an idea as preposterous because we know that more than knowledge of content and pedagogy is required.

This ability to relate to the youngsters and survive derives from the ideology and practices of star teachers. This ideology is a result of their life experiences and the growth they have experienced as a result of reflecting on their life experiences. This ideology can be changed but only by powerful, sustained life experiences as a mature adult which are reflected upon, not by the superficial and short-term experiences offered students in colleges and universities. Once individuals with the appropriate ideology are selected they can learn to be effective teachers by actually working as responsible teachers of record in poverty schools with the help of on-site mentors. As a result, the pools of teachers who can be effective with diverse children in poverty are college graduates with a range of work and life experiences who are more mature, typically over thirty years of age.

In Chapter IX, the star teacher's ideology is explained in terms of four basic beliefs they hold regarding the role of the school serving diverse children in poverty: stars believe that for diverse children in poverty succeeding in school is a matter of life and death; they believe in effort rather than ability; they value project teaching and thematic units more then they use direct instruction; and they have a great willingness to work in a problem-oriented profession. There are other attributes that undergird the humane way in which stars are able to relate to children and youth that many supposedly "fully qualified" teachers cannot. When I reflect upon what star teachers have told me over the last half century their basic decency comes through. Following are examples of human attributes which are not learned in formal educational settings, but which are typical of stars:

• They tend to be nonjudgmental. As they interact with children and adults in school settings their first thought is not to decide the goodness or badness of things, but to understand events in terms of why the children and others do what they do.

• They are not moralistic. They know that preaching and lecturing is not teaching and does not impact behavior.

• They respond as professionals and are not easily shocked. Horrific events occur in urban schools with some regularity. They ask themselves, "What can I do about this?" If they think they can do something, they do, otherwise they get on with their work and their lives. They respond to emotionally charged situations as thoughtful professionals.

• They hear what children and adults say to them. They listen and understand. They have exceedingly sensitive communication skills. They regard listening to everyone in the school community as a potential source of useful information.

• They recognize and compensate for their weaknesses. They are aware of their own biases and prejudices and strive to overcome them.

• They do not see themselves as saviors. They have not come to rescue the system. Actually, they do not expect the system to change much, except to possibly get worse. Their focus is on making their students successful regardless of the system.

• They are not isolates. They know that burnout can affect everyone. They network and create their own support groups.

• They view themselves as successful professionals rescuing students. Stars see themselves as "winning" even though they know that their total influence on their students is likely to be less than the total society, the neighborhood or the gang. They take pride in turning youngsters onto learning and making them educationally successful in the midst of failed urban school systems.

• They derive energy and well being from their interactions with children. They enjoy being with children so much that they are willing to put up with even the irrational demands of the system. Rather than always feeling exhausted, there are many days when they feel vitalized and energized from a day at work.

• They see themselves as teachers of children as well as content. They want their impact on their students to demonstrate that increased learning has made them more humane, better people not just higher achievers.

• They are learners. They are models of learning for the children because they are vitally interested in some subject matter or avocation that keeps them constantly learning. They share their love of learning by modeling.

• They have no need for power. Stars derive great satisfaction from being effective with diverse children in poverty. They are not motivated by any need for power over children, other teachers or parents.

• They see the need for diverse children in poverty to succeed in school as a matter of life and death for the students and the survival of the society.

It is not reasonable to plan on dysfunctional urban educational systems being transformed because too many benefit from their continued failure. The history of urban schools is that they constantly change by getting even worse. Individual schools, however, can be made effective, and countless children within them can be saved. The only way this rescue can occur is for schools serving diverse children in poverty to get better teachers who will stay. The teachers needed are available in every metropolitan area if we start recruiting mature college graduates and training them on-the-job. Just having more life experiences, subject matter knowledge and pedagogic knowledge are necessary, but not sufficient conditions. Teachers need the ideology and predispositions that have been described here in order to relate to their students and to bring their knowledge to life. Teachers are not born. They develop the appropriate ideology and relationship skills by reflecting upon, learning from and benefiting from their life experiences. They are not stars to begin with. Indeed, most begin as decidedly less, but they have the nascent belief system that puts them on the road to becoming stars and not the ideology that will lead them to becoming quitter/failures.

The introduction to this volume began with the statement "Issues of race and ethnicity undergird every statement on this page." Questions of equity and justice can only be dealt with by recognizing that racism is indelibly embedded in the fabric of our society and in the ideology of everyone socialized into American culture. The miseducation of urban schools cannot be understood as directed at only lower economic classes. Class is inextricably interrelated with race and ethnicity. For this reason the term "diverse children" has been used in combination with the term "urban poverty" throughout. Would our society permit 120 failing urban school districts to continue and expand if the only children in these educational wastelands were white and the beneficiaries of these failed systems were predominantly children of color?

References

Carter, S.Z. (2002) No excuses: lessons from 21 high poverty schools. Washington, D.C.: The Heritage Foundation

Corwin, R.G. (1973) Organizational reform and organizational survival: the teacher corps as an instrument of educational change. New York: Wiley

Dreikurs, R. (1968) Psychology in the classroom: A manual for teachers. (2nd Edition) New York: Harper Row.

Friere, P. (1971) The pedagogy of the oppressed. New York: Herder and Herder.

Garcia, E. (2001) Hispanic education in the United States. Lanham, Md: Roman Littlefield

Haberman,M. And Rickards,W.(1990)Urban teachers who quit: why they leave and what they do. Urban Education. 25: 3, 297-303

Haberman, M. (1995) Star teachers of children in poverty. West Lafayette,IN:
Kappa Delta Pi Honor Society in Education

Haberman,M.(1999) Increasing the number of high quality African Americans in urban schools. Journal of Instructional Psychology. October, 1999, pp.1-5

Haberman, M. (2003) Who benefits from failed urban schools? New York: ERIC Center on Urban Education. Teachers College, Columbia U.

Noguera, P. (2001) The role of social capital in the transformation of urban schools in low income communities. In Saegert, P. (Ed.), Social capital and poor communities. New York: Ford Foundation series on asset building. Sage Publications

Obiakor, F. (1992) Self concepts of African American students: An operational model for special education. Exceptional Education, 59(2) 160-167.

Payne, C.M. (1984) Getting what we ask for: The ambiguity of success and failure of urban education. Westport, CN: Greenwood Press.

Phillips, K. (2002) Wealth and democracy. New York: Broadway Books.

Pintrich,P.R.(1990) Implications of psychological research on student learning and college teaching for teacher education in R. Houston (Ed.) Handbook of Research on Teaching. Ch.47 pp.826-857 New York; Macmillan Inc.

Ross, A. And Olsen, K.(1997) The way we were…the way we can be: a vision of the middle school through integrated thematic instruction, 3rd edition. Kent, Washington: Susan Kovalik & Associates.

Ryans, D.G. (1960) Characteristics of teachers, their description, comparison and appraisal: a research study. Washington, D.C.: American Council on Education